What People Are Saying About

GW01006499

SLOW DANCING AT DEA

"This is an important book for men and women of all ages, but espe-cially for those with parents reaching their glorious golden years. I recommend Amy's heartfelt and practical book for my children, and I surely hope they will read it! It is also for anyone who wants to know how to approach this inevitable season with grace and dignity."

FLORENCE LITTAUER,
Founder of the CLASSeminar,
Author, *Silver Boxes* and *Personality Plus*,
Co-Author, *Making the Blue Plate Special*

"For everyone who, both present and future, will face the emotional turmoil and suffering of caring for an aging and dying parent, there is hope! With the passion and empathy of one who has not only stud-ied extensively, but, more importantly, has personally navigated these raging waters and found victory and healing, Amy Baker brings a voice of hope, compassion, and God's healing grace to those who find themselves Slow Dancing at Death's Door. *You know someone who needs this book—and she will thank you for it—even if that someone is you."*

DR. TIM A. GARDNER,
Author, *The Naked Soul*

"This book nurtures the soul of the caretaker! A must-read for the sandwich generation—Baby Boomers taking care of children and aging parents."

SHIRLEY MITCHELL,
Author, *Fabulous After 50* and *Sensational After 60*

"This book deals lovingly and honestly with end-of-life issues. It is insightful, inspirational, and practical for those who parent their par-ents. Thank you, Amy, for sharing your heart and your wisdom with so many confronted with these life (and death) decisions."

REV. MICHAEL S. BARRY, Director for Pastoral Care,
Cancer Treatment Centers of America (Philadelphia),
Author, *A Reason for Hope* and *A Season for Hope*

"Slow Dancing at Death's Door *is a unique and personal look at how we can care for and assist our parents across the finish line of life. Each chapter includes the author's touching experience, advice from experts in the field of death and dying, and God's promises and guidance during the painful times. Highly recommended.*"

KAREN O'CONNOR,
Author, *Help, Lord! I'm Having a Senior Moment AGAIN*

"*Amy captures the pain we all experience as we face the loss of a parent, and the upside-down process of parenting a parent. Masterfully, she offers hope-filled promise from her own experience as she outlines very practical principles to deal with a traumatic life event.*"

PASTORS CHARLES AND MARQUITA PATTERSON,
Church of the Hills, Austin, Texas

"*Amy Baker parallels her personal path of frustration, anger, and confusion with practical, professional insight, equipping you for your own slow dance. Whether you care for those in a 'before,' 'during' or 'after' phase, let this book be your dance instructor.*"

LAUREN LITTAUER BRIGGS,
Speaker/Author, *The Art of Helping*,
Co-Author, *Making the Blue Plate Special*

SLOW
DANCING
*at*DEATH'S
DOOR

AMY C. BAKER

LIFE JOURNEY®
Bringing Home the Message for Life

COOK COMMUNICATIONS MINISTRIES
Colorado Springs, Colorado • Paris, Ontario
KINGSWAY COMMUNICATIONS LTD
Eastbourne, England

Life Journey® is an imprint of
Cook Communications Ministries, Colorado Springs, CO 80918
Cook Communications, Paris, Ontario
Kingsway Communications, Eastbourne, England

SLOW DANCING AT DEATH'S DOOR
© 2006 by Amy C. Baker

Cover Design: Jeffrey P. Barnes
Cover Photo: Banana Stock/Super Stock

First Printing, 2006
Printed in Canada

1 2 3 4 5 6 7 8 9 10 Printing/Year 10 09 08 07 06

Unless otherwise noted, Scripture quotations are taken from the HOLY BIBLE, NEW INTERNATIONAL VERSION®. Copyright © 1973, 1978, 1984 International Bible Society. Used by permission of Zondervan. All rights reserved. Italics in Scripture quotations are used by the author for emphasis.

All quotes not cited from a published work are from personal conversations and correspondence with the author during February and March 2005.

Library of Congress Cataloging-in-Publication Data

Baker, Amy (Amy C.)
  Slow dancing at death's door / Amy Baker.
     p. cm.
  Includes bibliographical references.
  ISBN 0-7814-4262-1
  1. Parents--Death--Religious aspects--Christianity. 2. Adult children of aging parents--Religious life. 3. Baker, Amy (Amy C.) I. Title.
BV4906.B35 2006
248.8'6--dc22
                                        2005021920

To the memory of my parents,
Charles H. Croxton Jr. and Betty Wallace Croxton

CONTENTS

ACKNOWLEDGMENTS

❧

Preparing acknowledgments is like writing the acceptance speech for the Academy Award you never really thought you'd win. The names and faces are countless but precious.

First, I'd like to thank Florence and Marita Littauer of CLASServices, who believed in me, saw a glimmer of my potential, and encouraged me to pursue my dreams. The power of their godly encouragement is beyond measure.

I'd also like to recognize my friends at Cook Communications Ministries: Dan Benson, who graciously listened to my five-minute "pitch" on this book and somehow heard enough to pursue it, and Mary McNeil, my "first" editor. You'll always hold a special place in my heart.

I must acknowledge the "Impact Group" that walked most of this road with me as fellow believers and lovers of a faithful God: Ed and Cheryl Helbing, David and Lisa Hyde, Craig and Jeanne Parks, Scott and Kim Taylor, Marc and Carole Witmer, David and Cathy Tuohy, and Mike and Diane Wall were there from the earliest days of my difficult journey. Later, they were joined by Mark and Delinda Gillham, Jerry and Lisa Milner, and Mike and Amy Tipps. You all define what it is to love one another and hold one another up in the power of almighty God.

Then there's my intercessory team: mighty prayer warriors from several churches, including the prayer team at Church of the Hills. Thanks to you who faithfully read my e-mailed pleas for encouragement, inspiration, and discipline—then hit your knees for me.

I'd be remiss if I didn't thank the experts who lent their wisdom and experience to this book's contents: Jayne Gaddy, Dr. Tim Gardner, Rick Reynolds, Ken Parker, Scott Taylor, and Cathy Tuohy. I must also recognize Joel Quade and the staff of Parmer Woods Assisted Living—a Merrell Gardens Community—and also Hospice Austin. Their loving care for me and my folks during this season was remarkable. Their support allowed me to look back on a difficult time and write with only tears of peace and joyful relief.

If dogs could read, I'd acknowledge Valentine the faithful Labrador. She came into my life as a puppy when my dad was entering his final months, and she brought unconditional love, sloppy kisses, and many smiles to both of us. She wagged her tail graciously each time I celebrated the concluding sentences of a chapter and understandingly listened to me laugh, cry, and talk to myself when I was the only human in the house.

Two special teachers from my earliest decades must be recognized: Dottie Gray, the world's toughest English teacher, who first told me, "Amy Croxton, you are a writer," and Charles Duke, choral director extraordinaire, who taught me self-confidence and presence I didn't know I had.

Thank you, too, to the Meyers and Strasburgers, who graciously shared their weekend homes with me, far from the telephone and laundry and concerns of city life.

Finally, to my sweet family: Charlie and Karen, you are my biggest fans. Karen, I especially thank you for your childlike faith and oft-repeated, heartfelt prayer that "those people would *please* print Mommy's book." Charlie, you keep me in line. Thank you for the daily "Did you finish it?" questions and the reminder to keep it all in perspective with your "Don't forget to cook us breakfast," even when I was under a deadline.

Wayne, I wouldn't want to have walked this path with anyone else but you. I look forward with happy anticipation to the next adventures life brings us. I may be a bona fide, honest-to-goodness author now, but words cannot express how much I love you.

—Amy C. Baker, February 2005

PREFACE

As a businesswoman and church and school volunteer, I've spent many a meeting buried in goal- and objective-setting discussions. My former employer lived by the motto "If you cannot measure it, you cannot manage it," so I'm conditioned to think in terms of measurable objectives. I'm a list maker and *filer* (as opposed to *piler*, like my husband), so I've approached writing my books the same way. I have specific goals for you, the reader, as you explore the thoughts, stories, and suggestions outlined here.

Before we get to those, however, you must know the most significant difference between goal setting for this book and the corporate process I was so accustomed to: My objectives for you are inspired by heartfelt prayer and biblical principles.

To say that I prayed intently just to *get* a book contract for *Slow Dancing at Death's Door* is an understatement. God gave me a dream to be a writer when I was in high school. When I got married and took my husband's name, I immediately began using my maiden name for a middle initial. I just thought "Amy C. Baker" sounded like an author! When God began opening doors for me through CLASServices, the ministry of Florence and Marita Littauer, I prayerfully and earnestly began to pursue my dream to write books.

Psalm 37:4 tells us to delight ourselves in the Lord and he will give us the desires of our hearts. This process of becoming an author hasn't just been about perky praise songs and a cakewalk of a life. Arriving at this particular heart's desire came by experiencing a very difficult season— one where I found myself far from considering "it pure joy ... whenever you face trials" (James 1:2).

Dealing with my parents' decline and death brought anger, frustration, fear, loneliness, and grief. At times, I wondered where God was and why he wasn't answering prayer (at least the way I thought he should). In fact, one of those moments of desperation inspired this book's title.

We'd just endured another weekend of waiting for *the call* about my mom. Her condition had deteriorated again, and the hospice nurses didn't expect her to make it until Sunday. By Monday morning, though, she had rallied and was demanding breakfast and the morning paper.

"How long, O Lord, how long?" I slumped against the office door of the assisted-living facility my parents now called home and sighed. "Someday, I'm going to write a book about this whole ordeal and call it *Slow Dancing at Death's Door* because that's what I feel like we're doing."

No, there was little joy in that moment or in many others. There were times of little faith, too, but as I moved beyond the mental and spiritual exhaustion and dealt with the grief once the struggle was done, it became clearer and clearer that the situation I'd trudged through with much fear and trembling would serve a higher purpose.

One sunny July day, the proposal for this book had made it past one committee and was with another. I knew the final committee meeting was taking place that morning. I took the Labrador on her morning walk and talked with the Lord:

"God, please let this book be published. It will all have been so worth it if I get to tell this story of your grace, forgiveness, hope, and healing in the midst of what seemed like hopelessness and never-ending pain. Let them print my book, Lord."

Less than an hour later, the phone rang and my editor, a woman destined to become my good friend and ally, gave me the news all aspiring authors long to hear: "It's official. You're approved."

God had granted the desires of my heart. Now that I've started writing, my heartfelt prayer is even greater, even more earnest, as I seek to write not what I want, but what he wants. I don't intend this book to be a cathartic expression of my personal experience and a list of things for you to do, but rather a source of encouragement for you and of glory to the One who made life's whole adventure possible. Sure, there's a lot of my personal story here—you have to have that for context—but remember, this is not about me. It's about God.

So, prayer is the first dramatic difference guiding this book. The second is just as powerful—the Word of God.

Scribbled throughout my Bible are observations from various phases of my life. Written in the margin are notes of dates and events and special connections to a particular Scripture revelation. Some are downright amusing, like the notation by a psalm that says, "Mom's impending death. Nov. 1998." Bless her sweet soul; my mother didn't pass away until July 2001! We just thought it would happen so many times before that.

The Bible has been a source of inspiration (and some-times frustration) to me since I was a young teenager trying to make sense of my family and life in general. I've gone through phases of intense study and disciplined digging and I-wonder-where-I-left-that-old-book-anyway periods.

As I commit this story of practical advice and divine inspi-ration to the printed page, I pray you'll see how relevant the Bible's principles are to each season of our lives. Whether you believe in biblical inerrancy or understand how we got the Old and New Testament canon isn't an issue to me. What's important is that you experience how the Bible's inspired words not only convey God's astounding love toward us but also help for how we live today.

So we launch into this book. My prayerful, Scripture-inspired objectives for you, reader, are as follows:

- You'll see from my personal story how God, working in an imperfect family and within imperfect relation-ships, can inspire love and concern simply because we're part of his family.

- You'll discover how God can work miracles in the lives of fussy sick people and reach the depths of their souls with his unfathomable love. "For you did not receive a spirit that makes you a slave again to fear, but you received the Spirit of sonship. And by him we cry, 'Abba, Father.' The Spirit himself testi-fies with our spirit that we are God's children. Now if we are children, then we are heirs—heirs of God and co-heirs with Christ." (Rom. 8:15–17)

- You'll glean a few practical tips for caring for your parents and prepare for their inevitable passing from this life to the next. "Honor your father and your mother, as the LORD your God has commanded you, so that you may live long and that it may go well with you in the land the LORD your God is giving you." (Deut. 5:16)

■ You'll begin to be prepared—not just physically, logistically, and financially, but also emotionally, mentally, and spiritually—for this season of your life, knowing that no matter how messy your family is, there is boundless grace and freedom for you in God. "The Spirit of the Sovereign LORD is on me, because the LORD has anointed me to preach good news to the poor. He has sent me to bind up the brokenhearted, to proclaim freedom for the captives and release from darkness for the prisoners, to proclaim the year of the LORD's favor and the day of vengeance of our God, to comfort all who mourn, and provide for those who grieve in Zion— to bestow on them a crown of beauty instead of ashes, the oil of gladness instead of mourning, and a garment of praise instead of a spirit of despair." (Isa. 61:1–3)

Finally, I want to share the verse God gave me as I began my journey as a writer. At first, I was giddy with the news my work would be published. Then the reality hit: "People are going to *read* this. *Lots* of people! What could *I* possibly have to say?!" Therefore, this is my prayer and hope moving forward (if it was good enough for the guy who wrote a huge chunk of the New Testament, it's good enough for me): "When I came to you, brothers, I did not come with eloquence or superior wisdom as I proclaimed to you the testimony about God. For I resolved to know nothing while I was with you except Jesus Christ and him crucified. I came to you in weakness and fear, and with much trembling. My message and my preaching were not with wise and persuasive words, but with a demonstration of the Spirit's power, so that your faith might not rest on men's wisdom, but on God's power" (1 Cor. 2:1–5).

Friends, these are his words, his answers, and his messages of love for you.

—Amy C. Baker, February 2005

INTRODUCTION:
PORTRAIT OF A
SEMIFUNCTIONAL
FAMILY

She ate hungrily. No matter how sick Mother was, she could always mow down a bowl of ice cream after dinner. Dad, too. Before the late-night-show monologues had come to the last chuckle, they'd both devoured a few scoops of homemade vanilla to chase down their bedtime medications.

I'd begun to suspect they'd bought stock in a dairy, so I got each of them a personalized, one-quart bowl: *Betty's Ice Cream* and *Charlie's Ice Cream*. It ensured they'd keep their mitts off each other's munchies. We definitely did not need any germs being passed around.

They might not be eating well-balanced meals, I rationalized, *but at least they're getting some calcium and calories.* It was one in a string of rationalizations I'd started using since their health began to decline. I'd discovered that excuse making was a fine form of denial when things were progressing from bad to worse.

It's just old-age forgetfulness, I'd tell myself when I heard the same story for the third time in as many days. True, my parents were getting along in years, but the sad fact was that they were both very sick. Decision time was looming for my family and me. How long could they live alone? Should they stay in their hometown or move 183 miles down the interstate to be closer to me? Were they really taking all their prescribed medication properly, or did someone need to come supervise the ever-growing list of pills?

The questions mounted.

But I'm getting ahead of myself. I've jumped ahead to the final reel before you've seen the beginning of the movie. To really understand, we have to travel back a few years. Okay, more than just a few. *Like, to the 1960s, man.*

Long before the late-night bowls of Blue Bell ice cream, long before triple-digit prescription bills and a calendar full of doctor appointments, a baby girl was born to two folks who, by the standards of their day, were well past typical child-rearing years.

My father celebrated his forty-second birthday two weeks before I was born on a frosty night in early January. (I'd forever suffer through the combined Christmas- and birthday-gift curse only December and January babies understand.) My thirty-seven-year-old mother, who'd had a miscarriage two years earlier, found herself delivering a baby while suffering "female troubles" that would torment her until she had a complete hysterectomy when I was still in diapers.

They were on their own, these "older parents" with a rare only child. My few cousins were at least ten years older. The boys among them considered me a cute anomaly. The girls treated me like their very own giant talking doll. The children of my parents' friends also were much older and didn't have much use for a toddler bopping around our parents' cocktail parties when they were trying to play Twister and watch *The Twilight Zone.*

So, I launched into life as an independent, self-sufficient kid with a great imagination and a love for books and my own creative games. And my parents undertook the joys and pains of diapers, late-night feedings, and reading *Goodnight Moon* when they should have been looking at college funds and retirement accounts.

That independence—I call it the curse of competency—would both haunt me and serve me well in later years. As I faced the prospect of becoming an adult orphan at a relatively early age, I was grateful for that dogged determination and independent spirit that fed the I-can-do-anything-I-have-to-do tape playing in my brain. At the same time, though, I often found myself with my face buried in a pillow, asking God to rescue me from myself—to intervene with his hand … so much stronger than mine.

GOD MET MY PARENTS AND ME WHEN WE WERE ALL AT OUR WORST—AND OUR BEST.

This book isn't about me. It's about caring for those who cared for you when they can no longer care for themselves. It's about how God met my parents and me when we were all at our worst—and our best. It's about redemption and grace and freedom and forgiveness and an unfailing love that refuses to give up.

To tell the story in its fullness, though, you must understand the dynamics of this uncommon-yet-common family of the sixties and seventies. My life was much like that of any other kid growing up with *Gilligan's Island* and *Happy Days*. Dad worked in the defense industry during the height of the cold war. Mom stayed home and was involved in the community. We went to church (most of the time). I begrudgingly took piano lessons, and we went to the same goofy, wood-paneled cottages in Port Aransas, Texas, every summer to fish and build sand castles.

My parents loved me—perhaps desperately—and I was doted on but fortunately not spoiled rotten. They were quite proud of my average to above-average grades and "good girl" reputation. They were pretty strict and quite protective, and I was honestly too afraid of my mom's wrath to ever get into much trouble.

We didn't exactly put the *d* in dysfunctional, but we were far from perfect. On a scale of the Cleavers on one hand and the Simpsons on the other, we were slightly on the warped side of the middle.

As a child and young teen, I traipsed around to all the events my parents were involved in—which amounted to a lot of time in our boat, on the lake, providing courtesy safety patrols during sailing regattas. If it sounds nerdy, it was. But it was the life I knew—lying on the deck, bobbing with the waves, my bottle of baby oil and iodine mix nearby. (If you're not old enough to remember that infamous concoction, you might not be old enough to need this book yet!) I'd daydream and listen to the crackle of the marine radio and the background murmur of adult conversation laced with free-flowing, frosty-cold adult beverages.

To many of us growing up in that generation, the cocktail

party was quite familiar, and the theory that "it's five o'clock somewhere" seemed to pervade my parents' social lives.

It wasn't until I was older that I realized this wasn't healthy behavior. Although the alcohol consumption might have been *normal* (by the social standards of my parents' crowd), it was way beyond any definition of moderate.

It also wasn't healthy for my mother to make me her confidante about the most intimate and depressing details of her marriage to my father. Today, we'd call it TMI—Too Much Information. Sadly, she was never really happy, and she made sure I knew it.

As I grew older and got more involved at church, my spiritual life took on a new dimension. I realized God genuinely loved me and the relationship he wanted with me was personal to a mind-boggling degree. He wasn't just some heavenly grandfather or spiritual taskmaster. The church I was raised in had a dynamic youth group, and my fledgling faith became an increasingly important part of who I was and how I looked at the world.

Surprisingly, that growing faith was the first indication of the chasm that would eventually develop, especially between my mother and me. My religious zeal would lead to accusations, condemnations, and things said out of conviction but not love. (More on this later.)

Faith was different to my parents than it was to me, their

THAT GROWING FAITH WAS THE FIRST INDICATION OF THE CHASM THAT WOULD EVENTUALLY DEVELOP, ESPECIALLY BETWEEN MY MOTHER AND ME.

enlightened child. While I wanted to sing and shout and talk about it to whoever would listen, they'd been raised to believe their faith was like sex and politics: Something you don't talk about in polite company.

In high school I hit my stride and discovered my gifts: writing and musical performance. I was happiest when entertaining an appreciative crowd, whether it was musicals at church or Christmas caroling with the high-school show choir. (I even performed in the Don Ho Show in Hawaii! It sounds nerdy now, but we thought we were cool beyond words.)

My parents never missed a performance. Dad, the graphic artist, illustrated our programs, and Mom helped make costumes, usually hemming something as I was walking out the door to dress rehearsal. (She wasn't very adept at planning ahead.)

> I INADVERTENTLY LEARNED A CRITICAL LESSON: TAKE CARE OF THOSE WHO HAVE TAKEN CARE OF YOU.

During these years, I inadvertently learned a critical lesson: Take care of those who have taken care of you. Mom had a tough time getting my costumes finished simply because she had a lot on her plate. My maternal grandfather committed suicide years before I was born. When I was six, my maternal grandmother could no longer take care of herself and moved in with us. Mom and Dad built an addition onto the house so she'd have her own space.

I still remember carrying a tray of coffee and cream to her room every morning, pretending I was a waitress in some highfalutin hotel. I thought it was kind of fun to have Gram around, especially while she still felt like cooking. She made the best hot rolls in the universe, and I still remember the scent of rising yeast permeating my childhood home. For my mother, though, grandmother's presence added "caregiver" to her already long list of things to do.

When I was a teenager, my mother moved my grandmother to a nursing home. Her physical needs were beyond what we could manage at our house. Gram lived there until she died, right around the time I graduated from high school. At the time, she was the facility's longest-tenured resident; she hung on and on despite numerous strokes, falls, and close calls. Little did we know it foreshadowed the roller-coaster path her own daughter would take years later as she wrestled with her exit from earthly life.

It seemed like things were never quite right at that nursing home. A lot of old folks' homes were just places to stick elderly people until they died. There wasn't much talk about quality of life and rehabilitation and maintaining any semblance of independence. I still remember sitting at the foot of my grandmother's bed, wondering if she knew who I was, and hearing the deliberate click, click, click of my mother's heels as she marched down the hall to issue a new set of complaints and orders to the nursing staff. To say my mother took charge of a situation was an understatement. She *owned* a situation, and there was no turning her off once she'd launched her given mission. Betty could get stuff done.

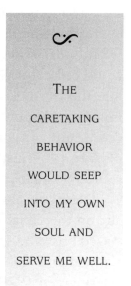

THE CARETAKING BEHAVIOR WOULD SEEP INTO MY OWN SOUL AND SERVE ME WELL.

Little did I know that the caretaking behavior I saw (and

was partially embarrassed by) would seep into my own soul
and serve me well when I'd face an army of doctors and
nurses later in life. I couldn't anticipate I'd someday be in the
same role as Mom, reeling in every inch of determination to
get to the bottom of yet another of my own elderly parents'
health-care crises.

By the time Gram died, our family had survived a nasty
head-on car wreck that nearly killed my dad and solidified my
mother's dependence on alcohol and prescription drugs to
get through life. She'd always been emotionally fragile and
prone to dramatic outbursts, and the tragic accident fueled an
ever-growing chemical dependence. It was sad to see such a
capable and brilliant woman sucked into a downward spiral of
depression and emotional instability.

In spite of her health issues and drinking, Mom was what
you'd call a functional alcoholic. I must emphasize the amazing things she was able to accomplish, especially in our
hometown's public gardens and cultural district. She was a
downright amazing committee chairperson and served as
president of just about everything garden and botanical
related for many years.

There was always food in the fridge, and dinner was usually on the table. During those frequently tumultuous years I
stayed busy and spent most of my time out of the house, especially after I could drive and zip around town in my scary
celery green 1970 Toyota Corolla.

By the time my college graduation rolled around, I'd set
my sights on moving not just out of the house, but also out
of the county. My life as an independent young woman was
just beginning. With a firm foundation of faith and an opti-
mism you only have when you're twenty-two, I launched into
life in Austin, Texas.

There's more to this transition story, but I'll save it for later. Fast-forward now to my late thirties. I'm happily married with two kids, a terrific church fellowship, and a solid, successful career, facing the rapidly declining health of the two fussy but lovable old people who raised me from the cradle. To complete the picture, I share with you now a bit more about the fascinating and complex people who raised me. Here are their stories:

MISS BETTY

My mother was smart, capable, competent, and tough. She was born on a farm in Tarrant County, Texas, and was one of the first women to graduate from the University of Texas with a chemistry degree. She loved to tell the story of her freshman chemistry professor looking directly at her and saying, "I'm going to fail as many of you as possible so you don't waste your time or mine in this program."

NONE OF US WERE QUITE PREPARED FOR HER CANCER DIAGNOSIS.

She rose to that challenge and many others as a community activist and staunch supporter of Fort Worth's cultural district. Every Arbor Day she did the children's sermon on the steps of our church sanctuary and over the years handed out a forest's worth of saplings to little tykes in west Fort Worth. She could make a mean pot of chili and cook brisket so tender you'd just look at it and it would melt in your mouth. Mom could sew a dress, rewire a lamp, handle a power saw, and grow a tree from a toothpick—and that was all before breakfast.

Despite all her positive attributes, she was neither happy nor physically and emotionally healthy. Although she knew God's love and Jesus' salvation intellectually, the message of hope and freedom hadn't seeped deep into her soul. Looking back now, she believed in God, but I don't think she really *believed* God and all the things he said were possible for her life.

Despite Mom's ailments and emotional issues, none of us were quite prepared for her cancer diagnosis in 1985. I'd been living on my own for a while and become less codependent than I'd ever dreamed I would, but I was no less stunned by the news. Back then, breast cancer was considered practically a death sentence, and hers was aggressive and already in her lymph nodes.

But my mother, famous for her steely determination and get-outta-my-way approach to life, decided to beat it—and she did. She drove herself to chemotherapy, then straight to garden club committee meetings. She wasn't about to let her impact on the city's cultural scene be dampened by a diagnosis of "the big C."

She perked along pretty well for the next few years but was always having some kind of operation. She had titanium knees, pinned toes, and really nice eyelids for someone in her late sixties. She had multiple doctors working on multiple things, supplying multiple prescription drugs.

After visiting us one weekend and not being able to recall much about dinner Saturday night, Mother decided to quit drinking. She called me Monday morning and announced in her matter-of-fact tone that one of my longest-prayed prayers had finally been answered. "What's that?" I asked, dubious.

"I decided to quit drinking." And that was that. She never had another drop. No Alcoholics Anonymous, no therapy, no self-help groups, nothing. Just sheer willpower and a tough mind made up.

I was thrilled. Finally, she would become Clair Huxtable and Carol Brady and Lauren Hutton all rolled into one: the perfect mom. Stable, smart, pretty, a good cook and house-keeper, and doting wife. All our troubles would be over, and she'd come to visit me, and we'd go out for tea and shopping, and we'd never have so much as a tiff again.

Then again, not.

By this time, her medication box was so full of painkillers, antidepressants, and antiseizure medications, she didn't need to drink alcohol to dull the ache in her soul. Still, it was one less thing to worry about and a great answer to many prayers.

In 1996 she went in for another surgery, this time to remove a bone spur on her neck. It probably could have been helped by physical therapy, but she opted for the hard way—it was another chance for a trip to the hospital and another surgical procedure.

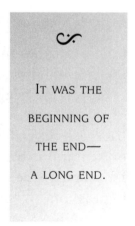

IT WAS THE BEGINNING OF THE END— A LONG END.

The surgery didn't go well at all. She emerged from the operating room with a paralyzed right arm and lymphedema that left her in terrible pain. The lymphedema caused her arm to swell like a giant sausage. The surgeon later said he'd never perform that particular operation on a mastectomy patient again due to the lack of lymph nodes, which help with circulation and fluid drainage. That, combined with nerve damage, produced a horrific result.

Betty had a brand-new granddaughter but only held her once. It was heartbreaking. She couldn't write. She couldn't fix her hair. She had to learn how to eat with one hand. I chopped her dinner into small bites when we would eat together, just like I did for my toddler. A classic "sandwich generation" scenario.

MY WORLD SHIFTED ON ITS AXIS THAT DAY.

Mom never really recovered after the surgery. The woman who'd never let anything stand in her way, the woman who beat cancer and fought city hall and ran roughshod over incompetent nursing-home staffers withered into a sea of deep blue depression and gradually became a recluse. The click, click of her heels was no longer heard in the halls of the garden center. The calls stopped coming for her to speak at garden clubs and ladies' groups. The little-old-ladies-in-tennis-shoes who held such sway over the cultural district had lost an important member.

It was the beginning of the end—a long end.

No one was really surprised when her cancer came back. I'll never forget that day. I was making an important presentation to the new vice president of my department. I needed to be on my toes and wanted to make a good impression. When 911 came across my digital pager, I knew things were bad. Dad never paged me anyway unless it was really critical, but those three ominous numbers following my childhood home phone number indicated something tragic. I excused myself from the meeting and ran to my cubicle.

My father's voice was a mixture of disbelief and devastation.

"Your mother has a tumor in her neck. It's malignant and inoperable." I sank into my chair and began to rattle off a bunch of questions to which there were no answers. She was so frail and reclusive and weak already, and now this? I wondered aloud what we'd do and how long we'd have before it was all over.

With my mind in overdrive and my heart on the floor, I went back to the meeting. I snuffled through my presentation, which now didn't seem so important. My mom was dying.

Here I was in another city, thinking I could just blissfully live my own dreams and aspirations as a wife, mother, and career woman. Suddenly, though, I faced an unprecedented kink in my reality. My world shifted on its axis that day and began spinning in a direction I'd never anticipated and hadn't prepared for.

It's hard to deconstruct and describe the years leading to her death in 2001. There were falls and infections, coughs that wouldn't go away, a broken leg that wouldn't heal, and this and that and the other. There were missed medications and duplicated prescriptions and angry outbursts contrasted with moments of sweet appreciation. There were outrageous long-distance bills, rushed trips up the interstate (it's a miracle I never got a ticket), and ambulance rides to the hospital. In short, it was one mess after another, with occasional interruptions of near peace.

"I DON'T HAVE GOOD NEWS FOR YOU, AMY."

Through it all, one thing remained consistent. My dad.

SIR CHARLES

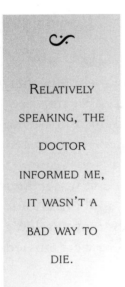

I don't know where my dad's nickname came from, but "Sir Charles" seemed to aptly describe the tall, distinguished gentleman who'd been gray haired as long as I could remember.

RELATIVELY SPEAKING, THE DOCTOR INFORMED ME, IT WASN'T A BAD WAY TO DIE.

My dad was a rock: even keeled, level-headed, and rarely bothered by much of anything. His greatest fault was letting my mother get away with too much in his ever-present quest for peace and harmony.

He and I sang in the church choir together. He puttered in his workshop and taught me how to handle a drill, a sander, and a soldering iron. Charlie never met a stranger and was quick with a laugh and a one-liner. He dotingly cared for his own mother who would, by the way, surprise us all and live to age 104.

Like most dads of that era, he worked a lot. He managed of a group of illustrators for a defense contractor. His job was top secret. I knew his company built airplanes, so I figured he and his team were drawing pictures for the owner's manuals of F-16 fighter jets.

When he wasn't working, he was boating. We always had a boat. It was our family's form of recreation and volunteer service. Mom and Dad were both members of the United States Coast Guard Auxiliary, the Coast Guard's civilian arm. Their mission was to promote safety on the nation's waterways. I learned to skillfully maneuver our thirty-three-foot, twin-engine Chris-Craft before I learned to drive a car.

Dad was a swimmer and golfer in college. He had a long, lean frame and had been remarkably healthy most of his life. He was nearing retirement and dusting off his set of old golf clubs when our world was rocked by *his* cancer diagnosis.

Prostate cancer—the old man's disease. It should have been an open-and-shut case—take it out, a few follow-up trips to the doctor, and annual checkups. But something else was wrong.

He lost weight, wouldn't eat. He kept getting weaker and weaker, and none of his doctors could figure out what was wrong. Finally, a diagnosis came through. Back then they called it non-A, non-B hepatitis. Today, we call it hepatitis C, and it's a nasty thing, especially when you're older and have drunk too much all your life. The blood transfusion he'd had during his prostate surgery was tainted. He was now a really sick man.

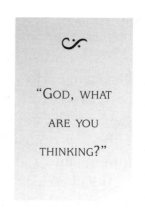

"GOD, WHAT ARE YOU THINKING?"

I was traveling home from a business trip when my dad's doctor finally tracked me down. "I don't have good news for you, Amy," was the concise but compassionate message. In his clipped, Pakistani accent, the good doctor laid out my father's prognosis. He had full-blown liver disease; the hepatitis C, combined with cirrhosis from too many cocktail parties, was a one-two punch that would slowly take him down.

Relatively speaking, the doctor informed me, it wasn't a bad way to die. Standing in the airport on a pay phone, I tried to absorb the reality that my father would likely develop dementia, then slip into a coma, his blood poisoned by toxins his dying liver would no longer be able to remove. "He'll just go to sleep, Amy. It won't be painful. Liver disease patients are typically very happy because they forget what's going on."

"When? How long?" I managed to mumble. It was hard to predict. Anywhere from eight to twelve months or longer, depending on how well he took care of himself, how he ate, other stressors in his life, and so forth.

I was numb. My poor mother's condition was growing worse daily, and now this. I stumbled into my seat on the plane packed with 231 other people, but I felt like I was flying solo. I'd never felt so alone in my life. My seatmates probably thought I was crazy, choking back sobs through a two-hour flight. No one ever asked if I was okay. In fact, it's amazing in such situations how human beings can avoid eye contact altogether.

"God, what are you thinking? Where are you? Why is this happening? How will I manage the care for both of them? I have two kids to raise, a marriage to take care of, and a busy career." The questions and concerns came as fast as the tears I tried to contain. I arrived home that night and crumbled into my husband's arms, sobbing into his shoulder.

I had no idea at that moment how many times in the coming years I'd leave smeared mascara and tearstains on my husband's shirtsleeves. My family's slow dance with death had begun.

PART ONE

Preparing: People Get Ready

*No matter how mangled our family memories,
how devastating our hurts, how desperate our
disappointments, the power of God's overwhelming
love can reach into our hearts' depths
and give healing and hope.*

PREPARING:
PEOPLE GET
READY

A sad-but-funny cartoon made the rounds a few years ago, showing a large auditorium decorated with a banner that read *Functional Family Conference*. Only two chairs out of hundreds were filled, and the lonely, bewildered folks were looking around the bare auditorium for others who shared their blissful family background.

It's unfortunate but true. Very few of us would claim to come from perfectly functional families. That lack of perfection ranges from a relatively normal number of squabbles and hurt feelings to all-out abuse, heartbreaking betrayal, and bitter estrangement.

When I consider my own circle of friends—people I know well to fairly well—maybe a third of them would count their parents as some of their best friends and supporters. What more could you ask for as you grow into maturity?

But among the other two-thirds are stories of wounds ranging from physical and sexual abuse and bitter divorces to custody battles and family disputes that were never fully settled. There are gut-wrenching betrayals that never healed and dramatic scenarios of flat-out abandonment. All told, it's a minefield of shattered hearts and broken relationships lurking beneath the spit-and-polished surface of adults who now have their own families, jobs, and roles in their communities and churches.

Many of us move forward into our grown-up lives and put our family baggage in a box, hoping to hide it in our soul's attic. We may marry and have a family or remain single, but either way we become focused on career and/or community, get involved in a church perhaps, and immerse ourselves in the rigors and routines of daily living. In our busyness we hope the family baggage gets more and more buried by boxes of Christmas ornaments, the LP record collection, a stored-away baby crib, and someone's rusting golf clubs.

> MANY OF US PUT OUR FAMILY BAGGAGE IN A BOX, HOPING TO HIDE IT IN OUR SOUL'S ATTIC.

However, certain events may cause that buried box to come to life. The shaky carton starts sneaking toward the attic door when a baby is born, a sibling divorces, a child graduates or marries, a job is lost, or another significant life event occurs. When that cataclysmic event occurs, the box is suddenly opened like Pandora's mythological box. Then the memory brings us back to a time when mother said something mean and spiteful or Dad never showed up to see us on stage.

Two events in particular can cause that box to explode.

One is coming to grips with our parents' mortality and becoming their caregiver as the end draws near. The second is facing their death, whether it's sudden and unexpected or long, drawn out, and debilitating. In this section, we'll explore what it means to prepare ourselves for this inevitable stage in our lives.

Someday we will all get "the call." It may be the stuttering announcement that a catastrophic heart attack has ended a life. Or it may be my experience: a call with a report of a devastating diagnosis that bodes a lengthy dying process. In either case, it means our roles and relationships with our parents are about to take a dramatic turn.

> IF WE PREPARE OURSELVES, WE'LL PROBABLY BE BETTER CAREGIVERS OF OUR PARENTS AND OURSELVES.

If we take the time, mental energy, and spiritual focus to prepare ourselves ahead of time for that inevitable shift in the landscape, we'll probably be better caregivers of our parents and ourselves. If we're married and have a family, we'll be more able to nurture our marriage and the children we may still be raising. If we also have a career to contend with, we'll be able to manage our job responsibilities and deal with the mounting pressure to provide for our family in a whole new way.

As you read on, you'll learn about my own life experiences, including phases of counseling and personal spiritual discovery. God used these coming-of-age epiphanies that happened over many years to prepare me for what I'd face in my late thirties and early forties. That divinely guided journey gave me a relatively healthy view of my parents as they aged and I assumed the role of their caregiver. It wasn't an easy journey, though. I'll honestly share the roller coaster of emotions and confrontations I faced with myself, my parents, and even God as I came to a place of peace with my family.

You'll also learn a bit of what modern psychology has to say about our family of origin and different approaches to coming to grips with the past. We'll examine several Christian counselors' observations from working with individuals and families facing both the past and the end, often at the same time.

THE POWER OF GOD'S OVERWHELMING LOVE CAN REACH INTO OUR HEARTS' DEPTHS.

Finally, we'll save the best for last. Read this and rejoice.

"The Spirit of the Sovereign LORD is on me, because the LORD has anointed me to preach good news to the poor. He has sent me to bind up the brokenhearted, to proclaim freedom for the captives and release from darkness for the prisoners, to proclaim the year of the LORD's favor and the day of vengeance of our God, to comfort all who mourn, and provide for those who grieve in Zion—to bestow on them a crown of beauty instead of ashes, the oil of gladness instead of mourning, and a garment of praise instead of a spirit of despair" (Isa. 61:1–3).

This promise from the Lord is balm to our souls. No matter how mangled our family memories, how devastating our hurts, how desperate our disappointments, the power of God's overwhelming love can reach into our hearts' depths and give healing and hope, even when we're slow dancing at death's door.

1

My Personal
Word on
Preparing

On one level, I'd say nothing can prepare a person for becoming an orphaned, middle-aged adult and for the process that often leads to that. On another level, I believe everything in my life prepared me to trudge the treacherous road I navigated. I'm a go-getter—an action-oriented, multi-tasking kind of woman—but I suddenly found myself overwhelmed and forced to wear even more hats than usual:

- Health-care manager

- Facilities manager

- Financial manager

- Estate trustee

- Property manager

- Personnel manager

And oh, did I mention wife, mother, corporate executive, church and school volunteer? There were days when I'd crawl into a ball on my bed and sob, "How much longer, Lord? Why is this happening? Why won't you let my mother die? She's so miserable!" It was beyond overwhelming. Our Bible study group patiently listened to my weekly reports that often sounded more like medical briefings, and we'd pray for peace and wisdom in the midst of suffering and confusion

OUR PAST PREPARED US FOR THE ROAD WE NOW TREAD.

Many of us look back on those seasons of our lives and think, "Wow, it's a good thing this didn't happen ten years ago. I wouldn't have been ready." Whether it's a midlife career change, the arrival of a baby, the end of a relationship, or a significant spiritual discovery, we see how the varied events and interwoven paths and journeys of our past prepared us for the road we now tread.

That's how I feel about the season when my parents were so sick and then died just fourteen months apart. In the preceeding years, God had graciously led me (and sometimes pushed me kicking and screaming) into situations and relationships that prepared me to move into that radically different role with my mom and dad. By his grace I assumed that role, although I frequently felt inadequate, staggering under the pressure of two families with dramatically different needs.

We're conditioned to think life's problems should be quickly resolved. We live in a society that seeks instant gratification and crises solved in thirty-minute sitcoms and one-hour dramas. We tend to think that once we ask Jesus into our hearts, life becomes a cakewalk accompanied by angels and praise music. But experience is rarely like that. Nothing is that simple.

Hebrews 10:14 says, "Because by one sacrifice he has made perfect forever those who are being made holy." Note the change in tense? We *were* made perfect forever through Christ's sacrifice, but we *are being* made holy. As my husband says, "We're all in process." Looking back on my own process, I see how God used different situations, events, and people in my life to make me who I am today. And hallelujah, he's not done yet!

THIS GROWTH PROCESS IS VITALLY IMPORTANT.

I believe this growth process is vitally important to us as we face the mortality of those who raised us. That process starts with an honest, gut-wrenching look, not at *their* issues but at ours. Here's how it happened for me:

I mentioned realizing my home life wasn't what you saw on TV sitcoms. There was too much alcohol. My mom's negativity was counterbalanced by my dad's happy-go-lucky-never-confront-anything coping skills. Pent-up anger would explode periodically; at the same time a fear of conflict contributed to create a walking-on-eggshells kind of world. In short, we were a case study in mild dysfunctionality and codependency, carefully skating around each other's issues in an attempt not to upset the apple cart.

It wasn't all bad, though. Back as far as my high-school days, God was providing graciously for me. I was involved in a dynamic youth group. Mom and Dad faithfully made sure I got there, even if it meant leaving a party at the lake early. Our church's teens were immersed in Bible and book studies, purely fun fellowships, and the constant message of God's inestimable love for us.

Our talented youth director was a gifted musician, and we performed contemporary musicals that she wrote, singing our praises and love for Jesus. I sang in the adult choir, too, and— in a riotous example of musical diversity—also learned Bach and Handel and sang over and over again the Scripture-based classic choral works proclaiming the majesty and wonder of God's love for humankind.

Steeped in this music—but also listening to Second Chapter of Acts, the Imperials, and wearing out Amy Grant's first album—I heard the message over and over again and sang it myself: *No matter what, God loves me, he has a purpose for me, and he sent Jesus to prove it.*

The message permeated my soul, even at a young age. When the normal tensions of being a growing-into-independence teen collided with home dysfunctions, my spiritual grounding made it all more tolerable.

On top of the message of God's unconditional love, there was also a theology in both my church and home that all things work together for a reason. In spite of her inability to console herself, my mother often managed to console me when the seemingly earth-shattering events of adolescence hit me. From my earliest Bible study days, I leaned on Romans 8:28: "And we know that in all things God works for the good of those who love him, who have been called according to his purpose." Mom had her own paraphrase of that verse—

"Honey, it'll all work out for the best"—and it was a message I took to heart.

A family legend illustrates this philosophy well. My paternal grandfather died when I was a toddler. I don't remember him at all, but know from the stories told by my family that he was a beloved, godly man with a heart full of love for the Lord, his family, and sacred music. As Papa was taking his last breaths, my aunt—his eldest daughter—remarked, "I know we're not supposed to question the good Lord, but I wonder, has he really thought through this?"

Yes, thankfully there was plenty of room in my family for God and acknowledgment of his working in our lives, especially on my father's side of the tree. And when we didn't understand life, there was room to question him. He was big enough for that.

Did I occasionally forget all that and slide into self-pity and depression and anger? Did I occasionally fixate on everything that was wrong and nothing that was right? Absolutely, but there was the exhortation to press on. After all, if Paul could write from jail, "I press on toward the goal to win the prize for which God has called me heavenward in Christ Jesus" (Phil. 3:14), I could press on through another evening worried about my mom's drinking and wondering when Dad would ever get home from work.

One of my most formidable spiritual experiences occurred when I went to eastern Texas to work at Pine Cove, a

> "I PRESS ON TOWARD THE GOAL TO WIN THE PRIZE FOR WHICH GOD HAS CALLED ME HEAVENWARD IN CHRIST JESUS."

Christian youth camp, during my college years. I spent two summers there, meeting people who walked passionately with the Lord and studying his Word in greater depth than I ever had before. It was a true life-changing experience. I was pulled, stretched, and jostled out of my comfort zone and challenged to take my relationship with God to an even more personal level.

During this time, I realized my faith was my own. Yes, it was the "faith of my fathers," but I was responsible for it, and my walk with God had to take a higher priority. Like the lame man who could suddenly walk, I was ready to leap back home and tell Mom and Dad all about my remarkable revelations.

At the same time, I went through my first real wave of self-discovery, emotional healing, or whatever you want to label it. Until then, I'd either just coped with or ignored the implications of growing up in my semidysfunctional home. Now that I was a fledgling youth worker genuinely trying to grow into a good leader by God's grace, it was time to seriously deal with some garbage in my heart and soul. I saw the sin harbored there in both the legitimate and overexaggerated stories of how my parents hurt me.

I also recognized the need to forgive them for the wrongs done due to nothing more than their human shortcomings. My motivations were okay, but my methodology was way off base. Knowledge without wisdom is a dangerous combination. Ever the writer, I proceeded to let them know in a letter how they had hurt me, how much (especially) Mother's alcohol use was out of control, and why this new brand of Christianity I'd found was so much better than the one in which I'd been raised.

I do not recommend this approach.

Looking back, the whole letter idea was ridiculously

arrogant and incredibly selfish on my part. My parents didn't speak to me for about two weeks. We'd never had a blowup like that before.

Once things were mended and I'd apologized for my dramatically failed attempt at relational healing and my overly zealous evangelism, we reached a point where we just did not talk about "religion" anymore. It became taboo, especially between my mother and me. I went back to counting the days until I could graduate from college and move out, sneaking off to Al-Anon meetings (for those who struggle in the shadow of alcoholism) and visiting other churches periodically when no one was looking.

However, something happened during that messy few months. A shift occurred in my soul that pointed me more toward the cross. I was discovering my identity based more on what God's Word said about me and less on the home life I came from.

My college diploma became my ticket out of town. I'd been visiting friends in Austin and interviewing for jobs there, much to my parents' dismay. I wanted to move out, but they insisted I get a job and live at home for a few years "to save money." When I called from the Texas Hill Country to let them know I'd landed a temporary job and signed a lease on an apartment, they were stunned. Two weeks later, we loaded up their station wagon with an attic's worth of pieced-together household items and some borrowed furniture. It was the first time I'd truly stood on my own two feet and gone against their wishes for me.

They weren't happy about my decision, but they became resigned and eventually looked forward to their chances to visit me in the hilly green vistas of central Texas. Mom, the ultimate pack rat, began to brag that she'd almost fully furnished my apartment out of her collection of stuff. "The only thing we had to buy her was a gallon of milk and an ironing board!"

The next few years were thrilling. Remember the first time you were out on your own? New friends, weekend getaways, dates, job changes, and challenges. I was involved in a great singles group at a dynamic church under a fabulous teacher. During this time I entered the second wave of personal growth that God would use to mold me into a woman who would someday care for those overprotective folks I'd left behind in Tarrant County.

OUR FAMILY

OF ORIGIN

DOESN'T DEFINE

WHO WE ARE.

I don't remember what precipitated it now, but I sensed there was another layer or two of the onion that needed to be peeled back from my family. Through my church, I obtained a referral to a Christian counselor and spent several weeks talking through my hurts, disappointments, and questions. The result was a greater level of peace and acceptance of who they were and who I was as a result.

I began to see more clearly that our family of origin doesn't define who we are, and our parents—often victims themselves of previous generations' mistakes—are generally doing the best they can. Now that I'm a parent too, I'm keenly aware that babies don't come with instruction manuals and that we have to figure it out as we go along.

That often-quoted Scripture from my youth came back once again: Romans 8:28. "And we know that in all things God works for the good of those who love him, who have been called according to his purpose."

I couldn't change who my parents were. I couldn't go back and rewrite the past. Yeah, it wasn't perfect. They were human. But, yes, it could have been worse.

What's more, Jesus died for them, too. Although their faith might not look exactly like mine, it was, nonetheless, faith and it deserved my respect and honor, just as the second commandment requires me to respect and honor them.

LOVING SOMEONE IS DIFFERENT FROM LIKING HIS OR HER BEHAVIOR.

Another dramatic revelation was my father's removal from the pedestal I'd placed him on. I'd always been closer to him, causing me to have ridiculous expectations for how he should have responded to my mother. I had to let that go and let him just be my dad. I realized I couldn't define the kind of husband he should or shouldn't be.

To sum it up, I finally recognized that loving someone is different from liking his or her behavior. I didn't like things about my home life growing up—a statement many of us would readily make if we were honest. But I did realize I loved my parents and wanted the best for them despite their imperfect parenting.

I gladly wrote checks to my counselor from my minuscule bank account and read the books he suggested on grace and healing. I hung on every word from the grandfatherly, wise man who had walked with God a long time and studied human behavior for years. I heeded his advice and let God heal my brokenness. It wasn't all the healing I needed, but it produced a big ol' Texas-sized wave of peace that washed over my soul.

More waves of fear, faith, and change would follow. They wouldn't all be gentle and peaceful. Some would knock me off my feet and I'd land with a face full of sand. Here's almost two decades of events in a nutshell:

- Mom's first cancer diagnosis

- Marriage to a guy my mother didn't approve of (fortunately, she later changed her mind)

- My wedding—held not in the hallowed halls of my family's church but at our own church in Austin

- The solemn news I was unable to get pregnant

- Dad's prostate cancer in 1991

- Our son's birth that same year (God is not bound by medical science)

- The news I was expecting a second child (really, God is *not* bound by medical science)

- Giving birth to a daughter. I didn't have good experience with the mother-daughter thing. This was really scary.

- Surviving a marriage crisis that would land most couples in divorce court

- Job changes and career setbacks that unsettled my self-image as a successful and ambitious career woman

With each subsequent life event, another layer of the onion peeled off, another piece of my alleged competence based on my extraordinarily insufficient human talents would chip away, and I'd find myself falling once again deeper into God's everlasting arms.

I referred earlier to the curse of competence. In spite of all the exhortations to "walk humbly with your God," I tend to run down the street on my own, singing "My Way" at the top of my lungs. Then the truck hits me. Over and over again, I've experienced how much greater is he who is in me, and I've had to make myself sit and be still before God (see 1 John 4:4).

We women of the 1970s and 1980s were conditioned to think we could have it all and do it all and be it all and never get wrinkles. We were supposed to be a combination of Beth Moore, June Cleaver, and Cindy Crawford and possibly even a successful businesswoman, too. Plop into that mix a pair of sick and dying parents, and you have a set of expectations that would make even Superwoman weak in the knees.

The bottom-line message of my personal story of preparation is remarkably simple: God will give us grace to deal with not only whatever lands on our plate but also with the leftovers from last night's dinner. Whether our plate is English bone china or plastic, his power is made perfect in our weakness. The plate may teeter, but the beans won't spill in our laps.

The Lord allowed the layers of this complicated onion to

GOD WILL GIVE US GRACE TO DEAL WITH NOT ONLY WHATEVER LANDS ON OUR PLATE BUT ALSO WITH THE LEFTOVERS FROM LAST NIGHT'S DINNER.

peel off one by one. With each successive layer came a new level of forgiveness, acceptance, relinquished expectations, and freedom from my self-imposed prison of competence. I'm dealing with a supersized onion here. Like the sanctification process promised in Hebrews, we're not finished this side of heaven.

RELY ON YOUR IDENTITY IN CHRIST, NOT THE ONE FROM YOUR FAMILY.

I encourage you to examine your own life, especially as it relates to your parents. Rely on your identity in Christ, not the one from your family. Honestly look at the forgiveness that needs to be given (even silently) and the acceptance that must be embraced. Do it before you assume the role of caretaker or find yourself standing in a funeral home.

I pray you'll be able to look back on your life up to the present and thank God, as I do, for the people and circumstances that made you who you are today—for each season, the lessons learned, and times God was perfecting you, molding you more into his image. That identity, covered by his resurrection power and redemptive grace, is enough to get any of us through anything.

THE EXPERTS' WORD ON PREPARING

From the earliest of modern times, men have tried to explain the complexities of the human heart, mind, soul, and spirit. Most of us are familiar with the names of some of the best in the field: Sigmund Freud, B. F. Skinner, Carl Jung, Erik Erikson, Jean Piaget, Carl Rogers are just a few of the bright minds who have attempted to explain the human psyche. This mix of philosophers, theologians, psychiatrists, and psychologists has proposed radically varying theories on what makes us tick, how we got the way we are, and how to deal with it.

We certainly don't want to place all our faith in the theories of fallible men. Many of their ideas are even directly opposed to what God says about his glorious creations. Nevertheless, some general principles can be useful as we consider who we are in light of our family. There are bits and pieces we can mull over—especially in the family counseling arena—so we're prepared for the end-of-life issues we'll face as both we and our parents age.

There are as many methods for dealing with family issues as there are families themselves. In this section, Christian counselors with marriage and family therapy experience offer several approaches on how to explore the past to be prepared for the future.

> ℃
>
> GOOD
>
> COUNSELING
>
> COMBINED WITH
>
> GOD'S INFINITE
>
> LOVE CAN HAVE
>
> A POSITIVE
>
> LONG-TERM
>
> EFFECT.

This section doesn't replace good counseling. It may be enough to get you thinking but not enough to get you ready for what you may face, especially if your home life was less than normal—whatever that is.

If you feel you should delve deeper into this subject—not as a pity party but to pursue genuine freedom and wholeness—I encourage you to seek help. Many churches and community organizations offer a counseling referral network, and many therapists work on a sliding-fee scale. More people than you realize have sought professional help to grapple with deep, personal issues. Even men and women of faith struggle with confusing emotions and hearing the Enemy's lies over God's loving voice. Good counseling combined with God's infinite love can have a positive long-term effect.

As you prayerfully consider what "heart and soul work" you might need to do, I strongly recommend you seek a counselor who is willing to talk about spiritual issues and who will incorporate the Bible's ancient wisdom into modern therapeutic methods. Seek the guidance of someone who's not only trained in modern psychology but also has a dedicated reliance on God as he or she helps others.

In researching this part of the book, I spent time with several counselors and role-played with them. All four have different approaches to helping people with difficult family situations. With each, I started the conversation with this scenario:

"I'm a middle-aged mom, still raising my kids, working outside the home, and trying to maintain a good marriage. On top of it all, my mother is dying. I have to take some level of responsibility for her care, but frankly, there are days I really don't like her. Can you help me get to the point where I can deal with this and not lose my mind, yell at the kids nightly, kick the dog, ignore my husband, and become bitter and resentful?"

Another scenario could be the following:

"I'm a nearing-retirement husband and father. Our eldest daughter got married last year and is expecting our first grandchild. My wife and I are thrilled, and I'm trying to focus on work for just a few more years until our son is out of college. We can see the light at the end of the parenthood tunnel, and we're dreaming of buying an RV and traveling. But now my dad has gotten cancer. They don't know how long he has. It's terrible, but I feel like my life has been interrupted. I care about my dad, but we've never been that close. In fact, I've never really gotten over some things he said to me when I was in high school. Besides, he's relatively young—only seventy-five—and has always been in good health. When my mom died, it was from a sudden and unexpected heart attack. I didn't anticipate this long, drawn-out illness would happen. I'm not sure how to deal with it all."

There are many versions of the same story being repeated throughout the country as more and more baby boomers confront their parents' aging. Even the fortunate ones with fabulous relationships with both their parents and in-laws may need help when faced with inevitable care issues, decisions, sacrifices, and difficult questions.

In my visits with counselors, two fundamental themes arose over and over again.

The first was the need to accept our parents as real people and take them off the parental pedestal they've been on since we were toddlers. Secondly, if there's unfinished business, emotional baggage, and/or resentment, it's critical to deal with it now. Quite literally, there are no second chances.

Let's explore the pristine pedestal many of us have knowingly or unknowingly perched our parents on. We expect them to behave and respond to us a certain way. Those of us who are parents will recognize this in our own relationships with our children—we sometimes disappoint them without intending to at all.

> IF THERE'S UNFINISHED BUSINESS, DEAL WITH IT NOW.

"It's important as our parents age to find out who they are and how that differs from our perception of them," says Jayne Gaddy, a licensed professional counselor and marriage and family therapist. "We have to get a grown-up perspective of them and stop blaming them for falling off the pedestal we put them on." That tumble off the pedestal usually happens in our late teens or early twenties.

Kenneth Parker, a clinical social worker and advanced clinical practitioner, couldn't agree more. "As adult children, we must accept that, unless they were inherently evil, our parents were just doing what they knew to do. Remember, they learned parenting skills from their parents, and that was the generation that endured a world war or two and perhaps even the Great Depression."

"OUR PARENTS WERE JUST DOING WHAT THEY KNEW TO DO."

Granted, our folks' parenting skills might not have been perfect, but it's rare that Mother was intentionally being the wicked witch of the neighborhood.

"Not many parents wake up in the morning and think, 'Hmm, what can I do to make little Johnny's life miserable today?'" says Dr. Tim Gardner, a licensed mental-health counselor and founder of the Marriage Institute in Indianapolis. He encourages us to recognize that our parents weren't who we thought they should be and to confront our own unrealistic expectations. Sometimes the tension we feel is more about us and less about them.

This process is crucial because when we're confronted with our parents' mortality and faced with the role of caregiver, our expectations for parental perfection bare their ugly claws again. We experience emotions we thought were shoved well under the surface, buried under a lifetime of other, more pleasant memories and the busyness of daily life.

Aging brings its own unique set of personality quirks and behavioral changes. These natural changes may magnify whatever issues we already have with Mom or Dad. For instance, everything slows down when we age: how fast we process information, walk, sometimes even talk. If we tend to be impatient, we're headed for aggravation when we take our elderly dad out to do his Christmas shopping.

Gardner recommends an honest look in the mirror to see where we assigned our parents negative motivations where none existed. "Identify the top three to five reasons you think you don't like Mom or why you're bitter toward Dad," Gardner says. He believes this helps reveal feelings that are really trivial and perhaps illegitimate.

> ౿
>
> "IT MAY BE HIGH TIME TO FORGIVE THEM FOR NOT KNOWING ANY BETTER."

Is it really worth it, for instance, to still be mad because Pop missed a few football games when you played ball or marched in the band? The reality might be that he was trying to make a living so your mother didn't have to work. He was doing what he thought was right at the time, not trying to hurt your feelings. "It may be high time to forgive them for not knowing any better," Gardner says.

This can be an important exercise. So can identifying the things that really did hurt—words spoken or not spoken that caused genuine harm. Ken Parker often has his counseling clients write their parents a letter. "It's a gut-wrenching, all-out exploration of the hurts of the past. All the legitimate reasons we have to be angry." The kicker: We never mail the letter.

Gaddy also uses this approach in her work with individuals and families. "There is something so therapeutic about writing," she says. "We're able to express memories and emotions we might never verbalize." Gaddy also agrees it's usually not appropriate to mail that painfully honest letter.

"My rule when it comes to therapy and in helping people process difficult relationship situations is this: Does it really build up the relationship? Will it ultimately help make the other party whole or tear them down and create more pain? Is it essentially a godly response?" If the answer to any of those questions is no, then Gaddy directs her clients to keep it to themselves. There's no point in openly rehashing old junk unless it will ultimately lead to healing and peace.

THERE'S NO POINT IN OPENLY REHASHING OLD JUNK UNLESS IT WILL ULTIMATELY LEAD TO HEALING AND PEACE.

It's the lesson I learned the hard way when I was in college. My ill-fated letter, written from the summer camp where I was working, should never have been mailed to my parents. It was therapeutic enough for me to get it all on paper, then let the forgiveness occur between just God and me. That five-page epistle should have become kindling for that evening's lakeside campfire. It would have been better being burned in the fire of God's grace and forgiveness than searing my parents' hearts the way it did.

That's the bottom line for this process of digging up old family junk: God and forgiveness. He's really good at it— we're not.

"Only through God can we forgive someone who has harmed us," Parker says. We don't necessarily have to *forget,* he says, but we can forgive our parents and eventually assume the role of their caretaker because they're children of God, "*even if*

they're not Christians or we're not on the same page theolog-
ically. We pray for them and let our actions be a witness to the
merciful love of God."

Sound impossible? Well, remember
Paul's words: "I delight in weaknesses, in
insults, in hardships, in persecutions, in
difficulties. For when I am weak, then I
am strong" (2 Cor. 12:10). No, on our
own we can't possibly dredge up the past,
honestly view our dashed expectations of
parental perfection, come to terms with
our disappointments, and then forgive
them. We must have the power of God
working in us.

GOD DELIGHTS
IN DOING THE
IMPOSSIBLE
THROUGH US.

God delights in doing the impossible
through us, in us, and for us. Healing our pain is why he
came. "The only one who will never disappoint us is God
himself," says Rick Reynolds, a licensed clinical social worker
and marriage and family therapist. He is founder of the Affair
Recovery Center and spends his days helping to heal broken
marriages. What he finds in that broken marriage is often a
wounded son or daughter.

His explanation goes all the way back to Genesis. "We were
born into a world where our identity should have come from
our deeply personal relationship with God. Instead, we looked
to our parents—who also are looking in the wrong places for
their identity." The cycle has been repeated for generations.

"When we fail to move into a place of forgiveness, empow-
ered by God, we repeat the same cycle with our children and
then find ourselves as adults responding to our parents as we
did when we were little," Reynolds says. This unending roller
coaster keeps us from being effective caregivers for our parents

and affects our ability to be loving spouses and nurturing parents to our own children. If we are single, the impact is upon our special friendships and those we long to be close to.

Bear in mind, we're not recommending making excuses for our parents, but instead putting mistakes and disappointments into proper perspective and remembering our parents are fallible human beings too. "The goal is to get out of our self-centeredness and into our identity in God," Reynolds says.

Basing our identity in God and all sounds holy, honorable, and significant enough, but is all this digging through the garbage really necessary? Many of us create our own reality and enjoy maintaining it. The family baggage is tucked away in the attic, and we'd prefer to keep it there.

In fact, you might be thinking, "What good will this do anyway? My mom is so bitter and angry at life, nothing I do or think or say will help. She's just going to wither away and die and be miserable, and there's nothing I can do about it." (Those were certainly my thoughts.)

Well, here's a denial-challenging, straight-shooting message for you: "It ain't about them, honey; it's about you."

Every counselor I spoke to had the same message: Deal with it now before it's too late—and do it for yourself. "It is very hard to live with unanswered questions or know you could have pushed through to a place of peace and you didn't while Dad was still here," Reynolds says.

> WE'RE NOT RECOMMENDING MAKING EXCUSES BUT INSTEAD PUTTING MISTAKES AND DISAPPOINTMENTS INTO PROPER PERSPECTIVE.

"When Mom or Dad is gone, all bets are off," Parker says. The relationship difficulties between us and our parents may not have originated with us, but if years later we're hanging on to bitterness or anger or resentment, now it *is* our problem. It's our responsibility to wrestle it out of our lives with God's help.

RESTORATION IN OUR OWN HEART IS CLEAR AND LIBERATING.

Parker suggests we ask ourselves, "What am I getting out of hanging on to painful memories?" The answer usually is "nothing good." "When we refuse to forgive our parents, we stay in the role of little boy or girl. Our parents are still arming us to be on the defensive," says Parker. When we're in that posture, we can't possibly help them manage the end of their lives with compassion and concern.

Gaddy echoes this idea. "If a parent dies and you know you could have forgiven them but chose not to, you have to live with that forever. It's for our own freedom that we go through this difficult process." Again, Mom or Dad may never know the burden we've finally laid at the altar, but the restoration in our own heart is clear and liberating.

A final word: Please keep in mind that this prescription is for the average family with a somewhat typical assortment of wounds and brokenness. Physical, sexual, or severe emotional and mental abuse is another category entirely and should be dealt with appropriately. There's no shame in seeking help for devastating sins against us. This portion of the book certainly isn't intended to replace therapy by a licensed professional. It merely attempts to boil down complicated social and familial issues into broad generalities that apply to many people.

Perhaps you're now convinced it's time to rattle the boxes in the attic and take the dirty antique rugs into the backyard for a good whack to get them clean again. If you're fearful, anxious, and just beginning to move forward with trepidation … good. This isn't a process to take lightly—or alone. That's where God's Word comes in like a breezy north wind on a hot summer day. It brings a fresh perspective to our life's doldrums. Let's bask in that refreshment now.

We're hunkered down, hiding from what frightens and oppresses us, refusing to believe that God has called us to be warriors and victors over our circumstances through his strength, not our own.

THE INSPIRED
WORD ON
PREPARING

ᶜᵎᵔ

T here are two key biblical principles to soak in as we consider the task ahead. One is the wonder-working power God has given us, and the other is his inestimable desire to heal our brokenness.

First, consider that immense power.

Paul said it with great conviction: "I *delight* in weaknesses ... for when I am weak, then I am strong" (2 Cor. 12:10). He didn't say he *liked* it when he faced the impossible or that it was *okay*, but rather he *delighted* in it! I don't know about you, but when I come up against something that's a lot bigger than me, delight isn't typically the first emotion that stirs my soul. It's usually something more akin to sheer terror.

However, the Bible makes it clear to us that God is

abundantly equipped to work in and through us in all circumstances. See what Paul wrote, this time in Ephesians:

> I pray that out of his glorious riches he may strengthen you with power through his Spirit in your inner being, so that Christ may dwell in your hearts through faith. And I pray that you, being rooted and established in love, *may have power,* together with all the saints, to grasp how wide and long and high and deep is the love of Christ, and to know this love that surpasses knowledge—that you may be filled to the measure of all the fullness of God. *Now to him who is able to do immeasurably more* than all we ask or imagine, according to his power that is at work within us, to him be glory in the church and in Christ Jesus throughout all generations, for ever and ever! Amen. (Eph. 3:16–21)

WHEN WE TRY TO DO ANYTHING ON OUR OWN, WE'RE LIMITED BY OUR EARTHLY, FINITE POWER.

When we try to do anything on our own, we're limited by our earthly, finite power. But when we remember God's love for us—which can't be measured by any hardware-store yardstick—and rely on his immeasurable power that works within us, we have victory.

Don't believe me? Read Ephesians 1:17–21. The same power that raised Christ from the dead—conquered hell itself—is available to you and me.

I keep asking that the God of our Lord Jesus Christ, the glorious Father, may give you the Spirit of wisdom and revelation, so that you may know him better. I pray also that the eyes of your heart may be enlightened in order that you may know the hope to which he has called you, the riches of his glorious inheritance in the saints, and his incomparably great power for us who believe. *That power is like the working of his mighty strength, which he exerted in Christ when he raised him from the dead* and seated him at his right hand in the heavenly realms, far above all rule and authority, power and dominion, and every title that can be given, not only in the present age but also in the one to come.

> GOD HAS CALLED US TO BE WARRIORS AND VICTORS OVER OUR CIRCUMSTANCES THROUGH *HIS* STRENGTH.

Hello! We're not talking about nine-volt batteries. We're talking about life-raising power to change the course of history—yes, even our family history.

This principle has rung true countless times in my own life—not just when it came to dealing with my family and past hurts, but in marriage, parenting, career, and friendships. Time and time again when I have had rug burns on my nose from falling flat on my face, he has delighted in pulling me out of the pit I've dug for myself and demonstrated his power within me.

When we're overwhelmed by guilt, anger, resentment,

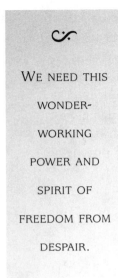

WE NEED THIS

WONDER-

WORKING

POWER AND

SPIRIT OF

FREEDOM FROM

DESPAIR.

doubt, and fear, we tend to hide. We're like Gideon, who, when surrounded by his enemies, resorted to threshing wheat while *hiding* in a winepress. An angel shows up and says, "The LORD is with you, mighty warrior" (Judg. 6:12).

Gideon looks over his shoulder (as if anyone else would be threshing wheat in a winepress). *"You talkin' to me?"* God called him a *warrior,* but Gideon so doubted his ability to be a conqueror and overcomer in his situation that he questioned this greeting. But he went on to lead his people to victory over the Midianites—not with a mighty, well-armed gang of soldiers, but only after God had whittled away the Israelite army to a mere three hundred.

Our lives are often a modern-day version of Gideon's story. We're hunkered down, hiding from what frightens and oppresses us, refusing to believe that God has called us to be warriors and victors over our circumstances through *his* strength, not our own.

Why does God do this? Why is he so quick to equip us, to send his armies of angels to our side with swords drawn to do battle against our enemies? Well, this is my favorite Scripture and it's applicable here:

> The Spirit of the Sovereign LORD is on me,
> because the LORD has anointed me to preach
> good news to the poor. He has sent me to
> bind up the brokenhearted, to proclaim free-
> dom for the captives and release from darkness

for the prisoners, to proclaim the year of the
LORD's favor and the day of vengeance of our
God, to comfort all who mourn, and provide
for those who grieve in Zion—to bestow on
them a crown of beauty instead of ashes, the
oil of gladness instead of mourning, and a garment of praise instead of a spirit of despair.
(Isa. 61:1–3)

Wow! Who couldn't use that kind of freedom and healing?
Apparently, God thought this promise was so important that
the prophet Isaiah said it about Jesus, then Jesus later said it
himself when he was teaching in the synagogue.

He stood up to read. The scroll of the prophet
Isaiah was handed to him. Unrolling it, he
found the place where it is written: "The Spirit
of the Lord is on me, because he has anointed
me to preach good news to the poor. He has
sent me to proclaim freedom for the prisoners
and recovery of sight for the blind, to release
the oppressed, to proclaim the year of the
Lord's favor."
Then he rolled up the scroll, gave it back to
the attendant and sat down. The eyes of everyone in the synagogue were fastened on him,
and he began by saying to them, "Today this
scripture is fulfilled in your hearing." (Luke
4:16–21)

Would that *our* eyes would be fastened on him too! When
life is complicated and getting messier by the minute—with
doctor visits; forgotten prescriptions; preparing for a sales

meeting; a slip and a fall and Mom broke her hip; and oh, we were supposed to take the kids camping—that's when we need this recovery and release. To embrace the role of caring for those who long ago cared for us, we need this wonder-working power and spirit of freedom from despair. We need it desperately.

Consider the passion in this prayer from Lamentations:

> I called on your name, O LORD, from the depths
> of the pit. You heard my plea: "Do not close
> your ears to my cry for relief." You came near
> when I called you, and you said, "Do not fear."
> O Lord, you took up my case; you redeemed my
> life. You have seen, O LORD, the wrong done to
> me. Uphold my cause! (3:55–59)

We all remember wrongs done to us. The recollections run the gamut from mere hurt feelings all the way to abuse and betrayal. But see God's Word—he tells us, "Do not fear." He took up our case and redeemed our life.

As we wrap up this section, we'll begin to move into the mundane and practical. But I encourage you, friends, not to let this exhortation to freedom and healing go unheeded.

One of the most significant Bible studies I ever partici-pated in was *Breaking Free* by Beth Moore. If you're willing to go the distance to be set free from past hurts, this is the study for you. Look for it online or in your local bookstore. And, gentlemen, it's applicable to you, too!

The Lord used this study mightily in my life, along with good counseling and teaching, to bring peace, acceptance, and forgiveness. He desires to do the same for you. He loves us so much he even lets us call him Abba Father, which means Daddy.

Our earthly parents may have made grave mistakes, but this heavenly Daddy wants to hold us in his arms and reassure us that we're his precious children. He'll never let us go; he calls us his warriors. When faced with the mortality of the earthbound moms and dads who raised us, this is nothing less than blessed assurance.

PART TWO

Planning for Everyone's Future

The secret of all victory lies in the organization of the nonobvious.
—Oswald Spengler

PLANNING FOR EVERYONE'S FUTURE

ೕ

I simply love to plan things. Parties. Vacations. School or church events, new corporate programs—you name it. I get all excited when I hear the phrase, "We need to make this happen." I shine when it comes to getting stuff done and I'm highly organized. The rumor is true—my spice rack is alphabetized. (Some of my friends, you know who you are, rearranged it once and threw me into a tailspin the next time I cooked.)

We've gone on long road trips guided by my trusty three-ring binder with a tab for each city we visit. In each section are driving directions, copies of our hotel reservations, restaurant recommendations, and discount coupons for local attractions I've printed off the Internet.

My husband calls this behavior obsessive-compulsive. I prefer to think of it as having the spiritual gift of administration.

One of my favorite Christmas gifts from him was a label maker. See, he harasses me, but I know he appreciates my ability to keep our little family organized.

That said, there are things in life that no amount of planning can really prepare you for. As an only child of parents who were willing to talk about wills and power of attorney and directives to physicians, I had it relatively easy. We took care of a lot of the details early on, and it made things easier as our situation progressed from bad to worse, then worse again.

However, all of my innate compulsive tendencies aside, things still slipped through the cracks. Oswald Spengler said, "The secret of all victory lies in the organization of the nonobvious." When it comes to caring for your older parents, there's much more nonobvious than you'd ever imagine.

> THERE ARE THINGS IN LIFE THAT NO AMOUNT OF PLANNING CAN REALLY PREPARE YOU FOR.

The purpose of this section is to acquaint you with both the obvious and nonobvious things that need to be considered and planned for as you anticipate your parents' golden years, which are often not golden at all, but gray and depressing as their health declines.

Oh, but this is so morbid, you might be thinking. Or, *I could never talk to my mother about writing a will! She'd think I was trying to get rid of her!* Certainly, these aren't easy subjects to approach with our folks, but it's worth it to push down that road now before things reach a crisis.

As I mentioned, my parents and I discussed quite a bit and

got many things settled well before their health truly began to fail. Even so, there were still issues.

We'll start this section as usual with my personal story. I'll share the decisions and roller-coaster ride of progress and setbacks that got my family to the point where 99 percent of things were taken care of. I'll mention lots of legal documents, possibly some you've never heard of. Don't fret. In chapter 5, "The Experts' Word on Planning," we'll go into more detail about legal issues that should be considered as you take on the caregiver role. (I promise, no legalese!) Then we'll close with some inspiring words from Scripture about taking care of the ones we love.

In appendix A, you'll find checklists and all sorts of handy resources for more information, mostly from the Internet. You should finish this section well armed with even more questions but at least with a plan, and if you're a fly-by-the-seat-of-your-pants kind of person, fear not. I promise not to try and convert you into a spice alphabetizer or loyal labeler.

However, keep in mind that you must have a bit of a planner in you or you wouldn't have bought this book! There is hope—even for those among us who'd rather "pile" than "file."

4

My Personal Word on Planning

After our first child arrived, my husband and I got serious about our own personal planning for the future. We pulled out the will we had thrown together when we first got married and owned nothing but some old furniture and Sears basement-sale appliances. We realized this dated document probably wasn't sufficient for a family of three with a house, some actual assets, and the meager beginnings of a retirement account. We turned to a trusted friend and estate attorney to help us get organized and prepared.

When I told my parents what we were up to, they were quite proud of our perceived maturity and foresightedness. I still remembered asking them as a young teenager what would happen to me if something happened to them and being relieved to learn they had thought through this unlikely scenario. I wouldn't end up like the orphans in the Boxcar Children books.

Now here was their married daughter making grown-up decisions based on planning and preparation they had modeled for me. It naturally led to a discussion of the wills and plans they had made for themselves.

My parents were smart people, pretty up-to-date on what was going on in the world. However, staying current on tax and estate laws is not a priority for most people unless you are a tax preparer or an estate attorney. And much of the information on this subject provided in the news can be confusing, especially to an elderly person who is more preoccupied with his or her own health concerns.

Such was the case with my folks. As they were settling into retirement and their growing personal health-care issues, times had changed. Medical-care case law, estate laws, and tax rules had changed. Laws dictating who could control what and make this or that decision were very different from when my parents were making their decisions. Their wills, drawn up many years before, were now woefully inadequate for their situation.

> IT'S A COMMON MISCONCEPTION THAT YOU HAVE TO HAVE A LOT OF MONEY TO HAVE AN ESTATE OR TO NEED A WILL.

These changes had nothing to do with the size of their "estate." It's a common misconception that you have to have a lot of money to have an estate or to need a will, powers of attorney, or any of those other fancy legal documents. This isn't necessarily the case. These are important documents for families of almost any financial means. And if there's more than one sibling involved or you live in a blended family with a complicated family tree, this planning stage is even more important.

Again, I'll provide a caveat: I'm not a lawyer. The following discussion of my experience is intended simply to get you thinking about things you and your family need to do. I also recognize that my situation was relatively easy because I'm an only child. So please remember that this short overview doesn't replace the counsel of a qualified estate attorney.

> ∽
>
> WE MAY NOT BE ABLE TO SECOND-GUESS WHAT MOM OR DAD REALLY WOULD HAVE WANTED.

"We pay you to worry, so we don't have to," we often told our lawyer when we were drawing up the necessary documents to provide for our children financially and ensure they were raised the way we desired in case of a tragedy. That's really the essence of this entire issue: what we or our loved ones desire.

When plans aren't made in advance and difficult issues aren't discussed before a crisis occurs, we may not be able to second-guess what Mom or Dad really would have wanted. This is the core logic behind how you help your parents talk about the tough stuff.

"Mom, Dad, we want what you want. We want to make sure decisions are made according to your wishes if for some reason you're unable to manage your own affairs." Perhaps it will sound like this: "When you're gone, we want to know how to carry out your desires for our family and your legacy. This is about you having control over this part of the future. We don't want to have to guess what you'd want to do with

Grandmother's china or Uncle Doc's antique rifle collection. Let's talk about these things now."

This planning business isn't just about money and material possessions either. It's also about medical care. My parents both made it very clear early on that they were completely opposed to heroic measures to prolong their lives. They also wanted their bodies donated to a medical college for research if possible. Talk about morbid! Sheesh! But it's what they wanted.

Face it, the older we get, the more we realize we are *not* in control over all things. As we age, we lose control over more and more things, including how effectively our bodies work. It's important to give our folks control while they're still capable.

> ℃
>
> IT'S IMPORTANT TO GIVE OUR FOLKS CONTROL WHILE THEY'RE STILL CAPABLE.

This is never more important than when it comes to predetermined decisions about medical care; lifesaving procedures; choosing a nursing home, assisted-living facility, or deciding to live at home; and what happens to their earthly belongings once they die.

Pop may be completely committed to his retirement account helping pay for his grandkids' college education—as long as they don't attend his alma mater's crosstown rival! Mother may always have had her heart set on granddaughter number one getting Great-aunt Mabel's pearls, while granddaughter number two receives the emerald pendant Pop gave Mom when he returned from the Korean War.

Planning is essential in both the mundane and the major, so I began discussions with my parents about their affairs while we were updating our own wills. Armed with all sorts of new (and only slightly comprehended) knowledge from our law firm, we began to draw up new documents for them.

PLANNING IS ESSENTIAL IN BOTH THE MUNDANE AND THE MAJOR.

Although I had a trusted attorney in Austin, I encouraged my folks to stick with the lawyer who attended their church and whom they'd known for years. I knew enough at that point to ask a few intelligent questions and ensure that everything I understood to be essential was provided, but it wasn't important that it was *my* attorney who pulled together *their* stuff. It was important to my parents that they knew the person drafting these important documents, and I respected that desire.

This is especially important if you live in one state and your parents live in another. You can't take your will, change the names and addresses and a few details, and have a valid document. Laws can be dramatically different from one state to another, and only a local attorney will know those critical differences.

My parents and I took care of three very important things well before we really needed them. First, their wills. Of course, as with most married couples, everything went to each other depending on who passed first. Then they designated a second beneficiary. Depending on your family situation, this may be more complicated. In our case, it all went into a family trust of which I was the trustee.

A side note here: For some reason we never named a secondary trustee in the unlikely event that something should happen to me. Fortunately and obviously, that wasn't an issue, but in hindsight, we should have done it. Once during our ordeal, my husband and I took an overseas vacation, and before we left, I hastily pulled together a notarized letter designating another trustee in case something happened to us while traveling. I had to make sure someone could take care of my parents' needs if I didn't make it back. It may sound paranoid, but sometimes a little bit of paranoia and a lot of planning go hand in hand to give you peace of mind.

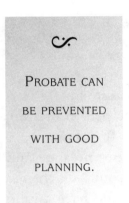

PROBATE CAN

BE PREVENTED

WITH GOOD

PLANNING.

While we were at it, we made sure I had signature authority on all their financial accounts and access to their safety-deposit box. These arrangements can create tension and conflict in some families, but it's better to deal with those issues sooner rather than later. Again, I acknowledge I had the only-child advantage; there was no one to argue with me over this or other issues.

We also made sure all their life-insurance beneficiary designations were current. Of course their primary designations were each other, but some folks don't realize there's often a place for a secondary beneficiary. This is a critical step, especially if your family has set up some type of trust.

At this point you may be thinking, "My parents have so few assets; this couldn't possibly be worth it." It is. Even the most meager estates are still estates. Going through probate to determine a will's validity in court is time consuming and costly. The process can also make personal information public, including financial-account numbers, Social Security numbers, and banking information. With the increasing threat of identity theft, keeping this information as private as possible is essential. Probate can be prevented with good planning.

Even if your parent has few assets—perhaps just a small Social Security income and a few pieces of furniture—it's still better to get Mom at least to handwrite whom she wants to get what when she's gone. A handwritten will is valid as long as it's signed by two witnesses.

Again, creating a will lets her be in control and takes away any second-guessing by siblings, children, or other relatives. It's also important, even when there's very little at stake, to grant someone else signature authority on her checking or savings account so any final bills can be paid with little or no hassle. And the bills still need to be paid! Creditors don't stop knocking at the door just because someone passed away.

You may be thinking, "My dad? Give me control over the bank account? Ha! He doesn't even let *Mother* know how much money he has!"

Approach the conversation from the standpoint of helping them *keep* control, not lose it. Help them realize you're not on a quest to take over, but rather that you want to help them plan now so their wishes can be carried out either when they become unable to care for themselves or they pass away.

Sometimes they'll surprise you. My dad had been fiercely independent all his life, but he was eventually thrilled to hand over the checkbook to me so I could take care of everything. It was just in time, too. In his growing confusion, he hadn't balanced his account in months and was seriously overdrawn. He was relieved for me to manage everything and would occasionally ask how much money he had. I'd assure him he was in fine shape, show him some bank statement balances, and that was that.

Here is a helpful illustration you might use with your parents: The U.S. Constitution provides that the vice president is sworn in whenever the president is unable to fulfill the duties of the office, even if it's just temporarily—such as when the president undergoes surgery. This carefully crafted stipulation has never led to an attempt to unsettle the authority of our great country. Discussion and documentation of "what will happen if" won't likely lead to anarchy in your family, either.

❧

Two other important documents every family should have in place are powers of attorney and directives to physicians. We'll discuss these in more detail later, but essentially they designate legally binding representatives to make decisions and conduct business on your parents' behalf if they are unable, for any of a number of reasons, to do so.

All this planning may not seem critical to you right now. Your mom and dad may be spending your inheritance traveling the world in tip-top health with no concerns whatsoever. But what happens when they call from Tuscany and need a check written or money wired? If you have a power of attorney in hand giving you authority to conduct business for them and if you already have signature authority on their checking account, then all is well. "We'll take care of it. Have fun, Mom, and don't forget to e-mail us when you get to Rome!"

❧

The final area of planning we should discuss has to do with the family residence. How long do Mom and Dad live in their home? Often, when one spouse dies, the remaining spouse is ready to make a move, and this can be an opportune time to transition to a retirement center or assisted-living community. It's a great time to downsize and walk away from the days of cleaning gutters and mowing the lawn.

However, other options can allow elderly folks to stay in their homes up until their death. One is a product such as Lifeline. It's ideal for the individual who can manage his or her basic needs but is a bit unstable and fearful of falling. It ensures help is on the way in case of a fall or other emergency. Some home-security companies offer a similar service. Folks wear a wristband or a pendant and simply press a button when they need help. The small, in-home communicator calls a monitoring service to send the appropriate help. This type of product is affordable and can provide needed peace of mind for both you and your elderly parent. It's an answer to that now infamous cry, "Help! I've fallen and I can't get up!"

WHILE THERE ARE MANY GREAT CHOICES FOR THE PHYSICAL CARE OF OUR ELDERLY PARENTS, IT DOESN'T MEAN THE DECISIONS ARE EASY.

There are also in-home-care services. Some in-home-care services are privately paid for by insurance or Medicare, while others are publicly funded by local or state government agencies and are available dependent on the need of the client. Careful screening and regular scrutiny are essential, though, to ensure that your loved one's needs are fully met. Getting references and referrals is essential. This relationship is like any other— the chemistry has to be right. We had to change caregivers occasionally when the personalities just didn't click.

WHEN YOU DON'T LIVE IN THE SAME CITY AS YOUR FOLKS, IT'S IMPORTANT TO HAVE TRUSTWORTHY "SPIES."

If Mom's or Dad's health declines and they need even more extensive help, do they stay or do they go? Do we ratchet up the level of in-home care or make a move? And then the question is where? To your house? Assisted-living or nursing home? (Very different places, by the way.) Then what do you do with all their stuff?

I mentioned in a previous chapter that my maternal grandmother lived with us for a while. My parents added a room to the back of the house, and Mother took on my grandmother's physical care. It took a toll on our family, but back then there weren't as many good choices as there are today. Eventually, when her care needs exceeded what Mom could give, Gram went to a nearby nursing home.

While there are many great choices for the physical care of our elderly parents, it doesn't mean the decisions are easy. In fact, this is the area where my family got stuck in the mud. As easy as it was to settle wills, "do not resuscitate" orders, and powers of attorney, it was beyond difficult to wrest them from the home where they'd lived for nearly forty years. It took a crisis to make it happen—and it wasn't just their crisis; it was mine, too.

By late 2000, things at my family home had gone from

bad to worse several times. Each "worse" was worse than the time before. There had been several emergency trips home, me zooming up the interstate to get to the bottom of yet another crisis. Mom had fallen. Dad had a sinking spell. It was becoming more and more obvious that a change was necessary.

For years, Mom and Dad had a ritual relationship with the Luby's Cafeteria five miles from their home. Soon they stopped dining out entirely, and Dad wouldn't even go grab dinner to go. He had stopped golfing with his buddies and didn't seem to do anything more than watch TV and toss water on the houseplants occasionally. Their housekeeper came every two weeks, and a neighbor made sure the yard was mowed, but other than that, typical household duties just weren't getting done.

In addition to concerns that they weren't eating well or getting out, we discovered my dad's blood pressure kept fluctuating. It would drop seriously, and he'd become unstable, dizzy, and confused. His blood sugar also was doing crazy things. This, combined with his progressing liver disease, moved my progressively weakening mother out of her league as a competent caregiver.

When you don't live in the same city as your folks, it's important to have trustworthy "spies." Family friends, neighbors, or an aunt or uncle can be useful sources when your standard twenty questions to your parents don't reap a satisfactory amount of information. My spies—the neighbors and a longtime family friend—called me frequently to report increasingly confusing conversations with my parents and concern for their well-being and safety.

At this point hospice had already been called in to help care for my mother. Mom had fallen and broken her hip, and that injury on top of everything else was a huge setback. This agency of angels—paid for by Medicare or Medicaid plus private insurance if there is any—is a godsend to the frantic family attempting to manage the constantly changing state of terminally ill family members. They provided someone to come in and help my mom with her personal care, a hospital bed so she'd be more comfortable, and oxygen when she had difficulty breathing.

Through local hospice organizations, I obtained a referral for an additional home-health-care provider to come in daily to help with meals and additional personal care. This was an out-of-pocket expense for my parents, but Paulina was a lifesaver for them and a boon to my peace of mind. She doted on my folks, and they seemed to appreciate her immensely. Mother had someone who graciously catered to her every whim, and Dad had someone else to talk to. Between Paulina, the housekeeper, and regular visits from hospice staff, it seemed our troubles were over. For the first time in a long while I felt like I could focus on my husband, kids, and job and not fret about what was happening back on the home front.

Until the phone call came.

Dad had gotten a little too confident after eating well for a few weeks. "We're doing so much better—I decided to let Paulina go!" he announced. "And we got rid of that hospital bed, too. Took up too much room."

I was dumbfounded. So much for thinking everything was perking right along. Have you ever been so mad at your parents that you wished you could ground them or send them to their rooms? My problem was that mine were already very grounded—practically housebound—and they didn't leave their rooms much at all.

On top of his decision to shut out the help, he had decided to have surgery for his arthritic shoulder. Anyone who knows anything about shoulder surgery knows it carries a long recovery process and you're basically incapacitated for a few weeks (especially if you're in your late seventies and have advanced liver disease). It was a classic case of too many doctors caring for one person and rarely talking to each other. And, of course, Dad wasn't really leveling with the orthopedic surgeon about what else was going on in his body and his home.

It took a "What exactly are you thinking?" conversation to get him to realize the surgery wasn't worth it and his body might not withstand it. I also pointed out he'd have to hire someone full-time to care for both him and Mom while he recovered. The surgeon, once apprised of the total situation, also agreed that surgery wasn't worth the risks. I never realized all the negotiation skills I'd learned at work would come in handy with my sometimes stubborn parents.

Here's an entry from my journal from around that time. I was distraught over the continued setbacks and frustrated that Mom and Dad couldn't see for themselves how bad things were getting.

My parents are in denial like crazy. Wayne and I are going to try really hard not to go up there and rescue them. I almost think it would be

THERE WAS A TRAIN WRECK HAPPENING BETWEEN MY HEAD AND MY HEART AS I STRUGGLED WITH WHAT TO DO.

good for some other near tragedy to happen so it
will knock them into reality.

It wasn't too long before I got my morbid wish. In his growing confusion, my dad took my mother's morphine and almost died.

Late one afternoon, I got another panicked phone call and headed to Fort Worth. I'll never forget that night. I vividly remember standing in a dimly lit hospital hall and listening to a doctor I'd never met tell me my father was in respiratory distress and needed to be put on a respirator. There are huge implications for that kind of decision.

I felt alone, confused, and like the world was falling down on my shoulders. My dear father was fighting for each breath, his blood pressure was dangerously low, and at that point, no one knew why. This on-call doctor, a stranger, was pressuring me to make a decision I thought had already been made. Dad didn't want heroic, lifesaving measures. Yet his quality of life up until that moment had been pretty good, and I stood there wrestling with a decision I thought I'd never have to make.

There was a train wreck happening between my head and my heart as I struggled with what to do.

God in his infinite grace gave me the strength to get through that night. I pressed the doctor to run more tests and get to the bottom of what was happening. (Doctors may look intimidating, but they're generally reasonable people who will listen to family members' concerns and questions.) I refused to put my father on a respirator, and later that night they figured out the source of his distress: the morphine. After a dose of an antinarcotic drug, he began to recover.

After that, it wasn't hard to convince him they needed

full-time help—if nothing else, to make sure medications were dispensed properly. Jenny, a registered nurse with years of experience caring for hospice patients, became a standard fixture in my parents' home. She had the perfect blend of skill, humor, and patience to deal with her increasingly crotchety patients. Once again I felt like life might settle back into a relatively normal routine.

Until the *next* phone call came.

"Amy, I can't wake your father. I'm calling an ambulance. You probably need to come up here as soon as you can." Jenny's voice reflected grave and genuine concern. She had cared for many dying people right up until the end, and she knew when things appeared to be critical.

Again, I put my life on hold and zoomed north. Racing up the interstate, I prayed my dad would hang on until I got there, and I listened to Twila Paris sing "God Is in Control" as loud as I could stand it. It was the only reassurance that brought any peace.

All the preplanning, all the early decisions and extra over-sight and care still couldn't prevent simple and unintentional human error. Once again, Dad had picked up Mom's medi-cine box instead of his and taken another dose of morphine. Even with conscientious caregivers, mistakes can happen.

This time, with my dad's liver in even worse shape, his negative reaction was more pronounced, but at least we knew what to suspect. A blood test confirmed the problem, and by God's mercy he recovered once again.

Now we began in earnest to try to move them to Austin.

It might have been different if there were more friends and family members left in my hometown, but there weren't. My dad had already lost his little sister to cancer, and his other sister and her husband were also in poor health and living in a retirement center. Mom had no relatives. I had two small children at home who needed me and a full-time job to reckon with. Oh yeah, and a marriage to nurture. On top of that, my parents' fifty-year-old homestead was beginning to show signs of neglect. The writing was on the wall. They had to move.

After much negotiation, we convinced them to fly south. I'd found a wonderful assisted-living facility that would provide much needed socialization as well as care for my increasingly tottery father, and we could pay for additional private care for my mother so she could be in the same place as Dad.

By this point, Mom had a broken arm and leg from another nasty fall and was completely bedbound. When you're not ambulatory—that is, unable to walk or otherwise evacuate yourself from a burning building—some assisted-living facilities can't accommodate you unless the family brings in additional privately-paid-for help. Mom was really at nursing-home stage, but I didn't want to separate her and my dad. It was an expensive proposition, but with Dad's pension, their Social Security, and proceeds from the sale of their house, we'd be able to do it.

I'd done my research on how to select a facility, conducted my own unannounced tour of the place, and visited at length with the staff. This was, after all, a huge decision. I was initiating a relationship with a team that would essentially become part of my extended family.

I breathed a huge sigh of relief.

Until the *next* phone call came.

"Amy, I just can't move your mother down there," Dad said. "It's just too, too much." I crumpled onto the bed in a fetal position and began to sob. My husband took the phone and literally took over. We were playing good cop, bad cop, and it was time for him to play the heavy.

"Charlie, we love you and want what's best for you. We're concerned about your safety and ability to live alone. We have to do something to get you into a safer place where your needs are met. This is killing Amy. You have to do this for her. We'll be there next weekend. You're coming to Austin." He hung up the phone.

Talk about tough love! There's no other word for it—it was *awful.* But there were no other logical options, and so we fully stepped into the parenting-the-parent role. The next weekend, we made the transition.

It was only a 180-mile trip, but it seemed like we were on the journey of a lifetime. As we pulled onto the interstate—the downtown he'd known so well all his life disappearing in the rearview mirror—Dad muttered, "I can't believe this is happening." I made small talk about friends of ours who were looking forward to seeing them and talked about his namesake grandson's baseball season, which was fast approaching. It was a feeble sales pitch, but under the circumstances, it was the best I could do.

"YOUR PARENTS WILL BE IN TOTAL SHOCK THE FIRST FEW DAYS, THEN THEY WILL WONDER WHY THEY DIDN'T DO THIS SOONER."

I was too exhausted and too relieved at that time to feel any of my own pain over the dissolution of my family homestead—that would come later. For now I was in pure task mode. I just wanted to get this done.

I drove Dad to Austin in their van, loaded with their clothes and personal effects, and we moved my mother in an ambulance. Wayne beat us to Austin by a few hours, driving a moving truck full of what they'd need in their new abode. The blessing of many assisted-living facilities is that you get to bring your own furniture and personal belongings. It feels a lot more like home away from home when you can sit in your favorite chair and finger your own well-worn remote control for your own TV.

Within three days, Mom was chatting with nurses and staff about *finally* being back in Austin where she'd attended the University of Texas. You'd have thought the move was her idea. Dad had found a dining table full of other happy gentlemen whose daughters also had ushered them into this new living situation. As they took their daily meals together and discussed everything from politics to baseball to the Great War, they often commented with big grins, "Daughters are dandy."

> NO MATTER HOW MUCH PLANNING YOU DO, THERE WILL STILL BE STRUGGLES.

It worked out exactly as the director of the assisted-living facility had predicted. "Your parents will be in total shock the first few days, then they will wonder why they didn't do this sooner." It was amazing to see these people who'd lived in the same house for more than forty years adjust so quickly to a new home.

To ease the transition for my mom, we kept the same caregiver. Jenny graciously lived at the facility for a few weeks until we found another group to provide Mom's private care.

At that point, Jenny tearfully said good-bye and headed back to Fort Worth.

We all began to settle into a new, much more peaceful routine, and my parents quickly became accustomed to seeing me almost daily, instead of just on weekends or when some tragedy warranted it. Grandkids got to make quick visits, show off school projects, and bring artwork to decorate Pop and Mamo's rooms. My dear friends, who had known my parents and their trials and tribulations, adopted them too and called on them frequently.

A few brave souls even occasionally took Dad to the driving range so he could stretch that arthritic shoulder and knock a few golf balls around. When he felt like it, he attended ball games and school performances. Once, my daughter's entire first-grade class went to Pop and Mamo's facility on a Christmas field trip to sing carols. Our daughter proudly pointed to her regal grandfather, who was so proud of his granddaughter he was about to burst his buttons. "That's my Pop," she said, equally proud of him.

The moral to this part of my story is that no matter how much planning you do, there will still be struggles. Unforeseen events and unexpected decisions will loom in the most unlikely of places. You'll find yourself on an emotional roller-coaster ride of thinking one minute the situation is under control and the next find it screeching into the stratosphere. However, with the right documents and decisions in place, the bumps are much easier to navigate.

As I handled the admissions process to move my parents

WITH THE RIGHT DOCUMENTS AND DECISIONS IN PLACE, THE BUMPS ARE MUCH EASIER TO NAVIGATE.

to their care facility, the medical powers of attorney and directives to physicians allowed me to sign everything and dot
every *i* and cross every *t*, so my parents could focus on adjust-
ing and making new friends. Times have changed even since
I went through this process, and it's important now to make
sure these documents include the up-to-date privacy releases
required by a recent HIPPA law.

Because our financial power of attorney included real-estate
transactions, I was able to sell their home within weeks to an
acquaintance—a single mother of two who had just finalized a
difficult divorce. I didn't even have to put their house on the
market. God provided beyond measure there; the only dis-
agreement between buyer and seller was who was more blessed
by the easy transaction. My family home is now spruced up and
filled with a new family making its own happy memories.

Because I was named on the medical power of attorney,
we were easily able to move my parents from the care of one
hospice to another and transfer records to a new set of doctors. Thanks to the Internet and branch banking, it was easy
to handle their finances—and again, I had all the documents
that allowed me to manage the transition.

As I write this now, so matter-of-factly, there's no way to
convey how extremely arduous this period was. Here's
another excerpt from my journal:

> *I have been to hell and back since late October.*
> *Mom and Dad are here now. I probably don't*
> *need to record the gory details of November. It is*
> *forever etched in my memory.*

Ripping my parents forcefully from the home they've
lived in for more than forty years—the only Fort Worth

home I'd ever known—was unbelievably difficult. But it was, nonetheless, the right decision for our family. Other families will make different choices about where their parents settle for their final days. There's no one-size-fits-all prescription for this choice. No matter how this applies to you and your family, this decision of where your parents will live out their final years is a doozy and can seriously test your faith (and patience).

I now know from experience, though, that good planning and a willingness to talk about the tough issues makes the necessary transitions much easier. So far, I've shared with you what we went through, how we managed it, and where we faced troubles. Let's take a look now at what the experts say about this subject. Time to call on the lawyers and social services professionals!

It's normal *to lose one's parents. The preplanning and foresight required to get all these decisions made and forms completed may seem daunting, but it can help ensure this end-of-life stage progresses with a greater sense of that normalcy.*

5

THE EXPERTS' WORD ON PLANNING

Whe you decide to march down this legal road, it isn't the time to call Uncle Jim Bob's third cousin twice removed who got a law degree back in 1965 but now owns a pawn-shop. Call in the professionals—a board-certified attorney who specializes in estate planning and probate law. You can locate one through your state bar association or talk to friends. Chances are someone you know has already traveled this path, and personal referrals are the best way to find reliable services.

You can do some research ahead of time on the Internet, but resist the temptation to download generic forms or buy a set of fill-in-the-blank documents from the local bookstore or office-supply store. Some of these ready-made documents can be a useful starting place, but laws vary dramatically from state to state. A tiny bit of verbiage in a legal document drafted in Illinois can inadvertently lead to a mountain of paperwork and expense in Idaho. It's much better to go the customized route.

GETTING SOUND LEGAL ADVICE TAKES ONE MORE THING OFF YOUR PLATE.

"You might save some money early in the process," says Scott Taylor, a contracts attorney with Armbrust and Brown, LLP, in Austin, Texas. "But the risk is that the documentation is not sufficient for your situation or specific enough for your state." That can result in exorbitant legal fees later, not to mention time and mental and emotional energy you really need to invest either in caring for your parents or in the grieving process once a loss has occurred.

Taylor doesn't practice estate and probate law (plus he's one of our best friends), so we know he has no ulterior motive in giving us this opinion! He does know a lot about good contracts, though, and the documents we're discussing are legal contracts. "Estate planning and wills comprise a very complex area of law. It's why we all specialize so much. Folks are much better off consulting a board-certified attorney who regularly deals with these issues and the constantly changing laws that affect them," Taylor concludes.

You wouldn't go to a brain surgeon if you needed knee surgery, so use that same wisdom when selecting an attorney.

You might be fretting at this point, "We can't *afford* an attorney!" Trust me on this one—it's worth the time and expense and doesn't have to cost a fortune. Many estate attorneys have "package deals" that let you customize services and products based on your family's particular needs. Some even offer update services so important papers are revised based on changes in tax codes and other laws each year or two.

In addition, most counties fall under the umbrella of a legal-aid organization that provides low-cost legal services to qualifying individuals. Again, you can search the Web for resources in your area.

I mentioned previously that in spite of my family's pre-planning, things still slipped through the cracks. There were two investment accounts we never put into the name of our family trust. In the grand scheme of things, the accounts didn't represent a lot of money, but I still had to go through probate to transfer those assets so they didn't just float off into a quagmire of legal wrangling.

Probating a will involves paperwork, meetings with an attorney, and at least one trip to the courthouse to appear before a judge. Depending on the case's complexity, it can cost well into the thousands of dollars. It's also usually a lengthy process. Ours was a relatively quick adventure because there wasn't much involved, but the national average time for probate is sixteen months.

Overall, probating a will isn't an *awful* experience—like getting a root canal—but it can be avoided if you're careful and pay attention to the details.

By the way—thanks again to the Internet—you *can* get a do-it-yourself probate kit. However, many of them still come with the caveat that their forms couldn't possibly cover all the nuances of an estate's details in every state. If you decide to manage this process on your own, be sure you've scoured every bit of detail you can find on the do-it-yourself process specific to your own state.

When you're facing the decline of your parents' health,

you have enough decisions to deal with. Getting sound legal advice takes one more thing off your plate so you can focus on your loved ones and your personal needs. On the other hand, attorneys can be a paranoid bunch—and I mean that in all love and respect—so use wisdom when taking their advice. We've ultimately made decisions several times on some nonessentials based simply on what made the most sense for our family.

The advice I've received from talking to "objective" attorneys (those who don't practice this type of law) is that it's worth it to have these all-important documents drafted by an expert—in the long term it can save your family time, heartache, and money. Hopefully, you're convinced now to get professional help. We'll go into some detail in the following list, but I encourage you to visit some of the resources mentioned here and the Web sites in appendix A. Your state bar association also will have a Web site with helpful advice and resources. As with anything, you'll save yourself time and money if you do your homework before you go into a meeting with an expert.

CONVERSATIONS SURROUNDING THESE DOCUMENTS SHOULDN'T OCCUR IN A VACUUM.

Described below are several potential documents that may be in a comprehensive plan. Each family and each situation is different. Many of these documents, while legally binding, can still be revoked or changed anytime prior to death or incapacity, so Mom or Dad isn't really setting things in stone. Some families are afraid of jumping into this process because they think they can never change their minds later. They can!

I can't emphasize enough that these documents vary from state to state. This makes it even more important to consult a qualified attorney, your family's health-care provider, or, if appropriate, a hospice organization to make sure the right format is used. It's also important to familiarize yourself with some of these sooner rather than later. When a crisis is looming and you're standing in the hospital hall with a doctor explaining all sorts of options, the last thing you need is the stress of trying to understand complicated legal documents such as do-not-resuscitate orders or living wills.

Lastly, the conversations surrounding these documents shouldn't occur in a vacuum. If you're the take-charge sister or the I've-got-it-under-control brother, make certain that not only parents but also all the siblings or aunts or uncles are reasonably involved in conversations about some of the sensitive issues sparked by these decisions.

WILLS

Wills come in all shapes and sizes, which we won't discuss; that's best left to the experts. Wills vary by state and are set up according to what's in an estate. The estate is basically real property (like land and homes) and personal property, which is everything else: cash, bank accounts, personal effects, and the lava-lamp collection. A will can do everything from specify who gets Aunt Fern's crystal vase to what charities your parents would like to leave money to.

Wills can be handwritten or typed and witnessed. A handwritten will must be taken to court for validation by witnesses who can verify that the handwriting is actually that of the deceased. There's a risk going the handwritten route because Cousin Lucia might want to contest the will after Grandma has passed away. A handwritten will can be more difficult to validate in court.

TRUSTS MAY HELP YOU AVOID PROBATE ALTOGETHER AND HELP SAVE ESTATE TAXES.

If an individual dies without a will, the state disposes of his or her property according to its estate laws, and that's probably not something that your parents will want. The law won't know your parents' wishes, so dying without a will may trigger an unwanted outcome, plus unexpected costs and delays may result. What those costs and delays look like vary greatly from state to state and estate to estate.

My parents used a living trust for their assets. While complicated, it might be a very logical option for your family. In short, it places all of a family's assets in a trust in which one or more of the children, a spouse, and so forth, are trustees. Trusts may help you avoid probate altogether and help save estate taxes. Talk to an attorney about whether this is a good option. Again, it may be expensive to set up, but it can save costs and heartache later.

STATUTORY POWER OF ATTORNEY

A statutory power of attorney names someone as the authority to make financial decisions for another individual. It gives the designee very broad powers and allows him or her to be the legal representative for a parent or parents in any business transaction specified in the document. The powers exist until that parent passes away. Make sure you get the real-estate transaction clause in there if you can. It's what allowed me to take care of selling my parents' house and immediately deposit the proceeds into their bank account.

Also, know that some financial institutions have their own powers-of-attorney forms that must be completed for each and every account at that institution. Check with your parents' bank, broker, or investment house to make sure you don't have to have a separate form signed and notarized.

MEDICAL POWER OF ATTORNEY

A medical power of attorney, which also ceases at the time of someone's death, is sometimes called a power of attorney for health care. It names an agent to make health-care decisions and access otherwise private documents. This power kicks in only when the individual can no longer make decisions for himself and the attending doctor certifies that lack of competency in writing.

This document has become more important than ever. Recent court cases regarding family members' rights to remove a feeding tube from a severely brain-damaged woman have highlighted the importance of defining exactly who can make what types of decisions. It's essential to choose someone like minded as the agent in a medical power of attorney, so the agent knows the wishes, values, and religious beliefs of the individual granting power over those decisions.

Remember, this document specifies medical and health-care decisions only—no financial ones. You can obtain this health-care form from most medical institutions, and it doesn't require an attorney or notary to ensure its validity. It must be executed by the individual giving the powers and witnessed by two people. It can also be revoked or changed at any time by the individual granting the power. It's a good idea to give your mom's or dad's doctors a copy of this document to keep on file in their medical records.

DIRECTIVE TO PHYSICIANS OR LIVING WILL

A directive to physicians (sometimes referred to as a living will) outlines an individual's wishes if a family is faced with difficult decisions regarding respirators, feeding tubes, and other life-prolonging issues. The contents of these documents vary from state to state. This directive takes effect only after a patient's physician determines that the patient is terminally ill and, that without any life-sustaining procedures, death is expected within six months. Due to the complexity and seriousness of these decisions, it's best to have an attorney who is familiar with your state's laws prepare this document for you or talk to your local hospice or health-care provider about it.

OUT-OF-HOSPITAL DO-NOT-RESUSCITATE FORM

You'll hear this called an out-of-hospital DNR. Don't confuse it with a living will. It's different. This is a very important document to have with you in original form if you ever take your terminally ill parent out to lunch or off on a weekend trip to visit Aunt Martha or if you have to transport Mom or Dad from one place to another in an ambulance or medical transport, as I did several times. This form—which you can usually get from a hospital, hospice, or other medical institution—indicates that Mom or Dad is terminally ill and requests not using specific life-sustaining treatments in the event of respiratory or cardiac arrest—or, simply put, death. This doesn't affect the provision of other emergency care, including comfort care.

Once again, this may sound odd to those not yet in this situation, but this document gave me great peace of mind. It allowed me freedom to cart Dad all over town on errands and even make that wonderful trip to Hawaii, knowing that if it was his time on some outing, no artificial measures would get in the way.

DECLARATION OF GUARDIANSHIP

A guardian or conservator is a person, institution, or agency appointed by a court to manage another's affairs. Each state has particular guardianship laws. In most states, to have a guardian appointed, a person must be shown to lack the competency to make or communicate responsible decisions about personal or financial issues. Age- or disease-induced dementia can justify a guardian. Only a judge can rule incompetence, usually based on a doctor's input, and this process can take a while.

Note that health-care professionals delineate a difference between competency and capability. Competency refers to an individual being adequately qualified, skilled, fit, able to make decisions, and so forth. Capability indicates the mental power to understand. In other words, Mom can tell you what form she's signing and what it means. Ten minutes later, she may have forgotten all about it, but at the time, she understands. Old-age forgetfulness doesn't constitute incompetency.

"We're from the Government, and We're Here to Help."

If you're taking on the role of caregiver for a family member, you're not alone. It's estimated that more than seven million people in the U.S. are informal caregivers, and between 20 and 40 percent of those caregivers have children under eighteen to care for as well. As we wrap up this expert section, it's worth discussing the many agencies that are out there to help you and your family with the choices, decisions, and needs that arise as you become a caregiver. Your tax dollars pay for many of these, so you might as well take advantage of them!

Appendix A lists several helpful Web sites that provide great resources and advice for caregivers. One of my favorites is A Place for Mom. This comprehensive site is a nationwide elder-care referral service, and it includes helpful tips to help you evaluate not just your family's needs but also specific care facilities.

The Social Security Administration's helpful site contains a tremendous amount of information and forms you can download. I've found its search engine to be fairly accurate, so you can easily find answers to your questions.

Another useful site is that of the National Association of

Area Agencies on Aging, or N4A. Its mission is to help older people and those with disabilities live in their homes and communities with dignity and choices for as long as possible. It also has an elder-care locator that will help you find agencies that serve your specific community.

For instance, my county's Area Agency on Aging office provides counseling to help families better understand the benefits available and to help individuals through the maze of government benefits programs. They also provide care coordination to evaluate what a person needs in order to remain independent as long as possible. This service also has support, training, and resources for caregivers, such as respite care so you can get a break occasionally.

The American Association for Homecare supports quality health-care services in one's home. This group's mission also is to help aging Americans remain independent for as long as possible. They have good information on helping select home-health-care providers and links to similar organizations that serve specific states. I mentioned earlier that we had to change a few times, and you shouldn't be afraid if you have to do this yourself. Since selecting home-health-care providers can become absolutely critical, good guidelines can help make the choice easier.

CAPS—Children of Aging Parents—has caregiver guides and interesting and encouraging stories from others who are in the same rocky boat you may be in. This helpful Web site is listed in appendix A too.

GETTING REFERRALS FROM FRIENDS OR RELATIVES WHO HAVE USED HOSPICE SERVICES IS ESSENTIAL.

Specific Thoughts on Hospice Care

✑

The National Hospice and Palliative Care Organization is a major source of information on those subjects. Palliative care is treatment that improves an individual's comfort and quality of life during the last phase of life without treating the underlying incurable disease. In palliative care the individual, physician(s), primary caregiver, and the hospice team agree that a treatment's expected outcome is relief from pain and distressing symptoms and/or enhancing the quality of life. It's the underlying reason why we quit my parents' chemotherapy treatments after a certain point.

Through this organization you can find out about hospice providers in your area and fully understand what they offer so that when your dad's doctor says, "It's time to call hospice," you're prepared to move forward. The group manages an especially helpful Web site specifically for consumers, www.caringinfo.org. Specialized hospice caregivers are a huge blessing for family members who often are standing by feeling helpless at this stage.

Many larger communities have more than one hospice provider, and you may need to choose between private, non-profit, or corporately owned hospices. Getting referrals from friends or relatives who have used hospice services is essential if there are choices in your community. Also, if you're selecting an assisted-living facility or nursing home for your parent, these facilities often have preferred hospice providers and can advise you on which ones may be best for your mom or dad.

You'll often hear statements like, "Now I can't advocate one agency or service over another ..." but when you press for information—perhaps by asking, "What would you do if it was your mom?"—you may get the inside scoop on which organization is best.

Staff turnover is a very important factor to consider in a hospice. It's very similar to selecting child day care—you want to ensure that the nurses, social workers, and caregivers who'll take care of your loved one remain the same for as long as possible. An organization with high turnover or frequent reorganizations won't provide the consistent care that brings both your parent and you peace of mind.

Finally, I've been asked, "Isn't there just *someone* who can come in and tell my mom she absolutely has to move to assisted living?" Sorry, but no. When we were wrestling with the need to move my parents, my husband told them in quite serious tones that the state could come in and take over unless they moved to a safer situation. It sounded good (and worked), but we later learned that it really isn't true.

The closest we can get to a mandated move is by using the guardianship process, and as previously mentioned, it's long and complicated, although especially helpful when a parent suffers from Alzheimer's or other forms of dementia. Begin to explore that option now if you think it might be the right one for your family.

FINALLY, THE FUNERAL

One last thing that I won't discuss in detail but must at least touch on is the funeral. My parents both wanted to be cremated. This may sound horrifying to some, but it was their choice and I honored it. Honestly, it didn't thrill me, but our family has never been one to go visit a deceased loved one's grave, so this decision did not surprise me and, in fact, seemed very practical. They didn't want "people gawking at us" or elaborate graveside services. Therefore my involvement with the funeral home was minimal.

When it was clear we were nearing the end, I went ahead and prepaid for the cremation arrangements and signed everything I could in advance so that when the time came there was less to worry about and I could focus on other things. If you are involved in hospice, they will have this information available through the chaplain assigned to you. I chose a large, family-owned funeral home in Austin with a stellar reputation. I asked around and got good feedback from others who had used its services. When it was all over with, my experience there had been as pleasant as possible.

This issue of prepaying for funerals is a tricky one. Some financial planners advise against it because prices may change over time. Prepaying may not be the most cost-effective solution long term. Like anything else, you should do your homework and rely heavily on referrals from friends and family who have needed these essential services. Make certain you're getting what you pay for and there are no hidden costs for necessary elements, like a trip from where the individual died to the funeral home, that are not mentioned in the prepaid contract. The "peace of mind" notion that sells many on the prepayment idea goes out the window when you discover in the midst of your grief that all the expenses aren't really covered.

This whole subject reminds me of two amusing stories.

When my paternal grandfather died, he'd suffered from cancer for quite a while and didn't look like himself by the time he went to his heavenly home. My grandmother, feeling the inevitable mix of grief and relief, didn't want to go to the funeral home for the viewing.

Her children insisted. "Mama, he looks good. Very handsome and peaceful," my dad told her. She relented. They drove to the funeral home, located in a beautiful old mansion near downtown Fort Worth. Guy Thompson, a second-generation funeral director, had taken care of other services for my family, and the Croxton legacy held a special place in his heart. In fact he and my father were old high-school classmates.

My grandmother went tentatively into the family room and peered into the casket, where she saw her beloved husband resting. He looked so much like himself, so much more at peace than she had imagined, that she exclaimed, "Well, Guy, he looks wonderful! I can't *wait* for you to get a hold of me!"

On the other side of the family tree, when my husband's grandmother was nearing the end of her life, she went with her daughters to the funeral home to make her choices and ensure her wishes were carried out. You couldn't get things simple enough for this feisty Texan who'd lived her eighty-two years *her way* and wasn't about to change now.

"Put me in a cardboard box and shut the lid!" she insisted. "And I don't want people staring at me once I'm gone." There would be no formal, flower-filled funeral service for her. As the discussion progressed with the funeral-home staff, she was horrified to learn there was a charge for everything from a trip in the hearse to having the inevitable hole dug at the gravesite. This old Irish soul had

"INVESTING IN THESE DECISIONS AND THIS PREPARATION EARLY PAYS OFF DRAMATICALLY."

immense faith in God and was ready to go home without fanfare or unnecessary expense.

"I don't want to pay for a ride in a hearse," she said. One of her daughters jokingly offered to borrow a pickup truck. When the laughter died down, the speechless funeral director left the room to consult with his superiors. Finally, they all agreed that when the day came, they would transport her in the funeral home's van. It wouldn't be a luxurious trip, but that's what this plainspoken little lady wanted. If she'd thought of it, she probably would have suggested her daughters bring their own shovels to the cemetery.

A few weeks later, this dear little lady was dying in the hospital. Her family was gathered around and had brought a CD player to fill her final moments with her favorite Gaither Vocal Band tunes. Apparently she felt like it was a bit too much commotion. She sat up in bed with energy that had been absent for days and demanded, *"Turn that off! You're making too much noise!"* With that she laid her head down on her pillow, closed her eyes, and was gone.

She got in the last word. Her family was able to enjoy those last moments with her, and right before she died, they saw a glimpse of the lively spirit that had marked her life. With all the planning completed, there was nothing left to do but hug and weep and celebrate a life well lived. Would that we all could go someday, surrounded by our loving family, having the last word as she did!

༄

Whew! That's a lot, isn't it? There are a multitude of decisions—and, fortunately, a plethora of resources to choose from. As they say, the only certain things in life are death and taxes. It's also certain that neither is simple.

"Investing in these decisions and this preparation early pays off dramatically when a family finally reaches this inevitable stage in life's journey," says Brad Wiewel, a board-certified attorney specializing in estate planning and probate law. "Our firm has seen so many cases where end-of-life issues were faced with greater peace and dignity because tough conversations had already taken place."

Like many other estate lawyers, Wiewel is a member of the National Network of Estate Planning Attorneys. They give state-of-the-art and up-to-the-minute advice to clients in a field of law that is ever changing.

"Estate planning is a unique combination of using the rational mind, which knows what to do with information, and the compassionate mind, which deals with a family's unique set of emotions and struggles," Wiewel says. An experienced firm that's comfortable with uncomfortable subjects can make the necessary planning easier than most realize.

Cathy Tuohy, a social worker with years of hospice experience, has seen her fair share of families facing the end of a parent's life. "When people have done the tough work up front," she says, "the end can be so much less complicated. Families are able to focus on both the loved one's needs and theirs and not worry about all the legal issues that surround elder-care decisions and ultimately a family member's death."

She reminds her families that it's *normal* to lose one's parents. The preplanning and foresight required to get all these decisions made and forms completed may seem daunting, but it can help ensure this end-of-life stage progresses with a greater sense of that normalcy.

Tuohy recalls complicated family situations made all the

more thorny when the difficult questions were ignored. "It's like the proverbial elephant in the middle of the room. Everyone knows it's there, but no one has dealt with it yet. Lack of planning prevents a family from being able to effectively manage the roller coaster of emotions that come with an impending loss."

We've seen the compelling arguments for preplanning and having the hard conversations early in the process we'll all face. These preplanning experts have shared their advice based on their training and experience. But what does the Bible say? Is there a scriptural mandate for this planning and preparation?

Those ancient words were written well before the days of lawyers, privacy laws, and complex medical procedures. But there's definitely wisdom there to guide us as we care for those we love in their final days.

THE INSPIRED
WORD ON
PLANNING

Wednesday read far into the Bible to find the first words written about caring for our parents: "Honor your father and your mother, so that you may live long in the land the LORD your God is giving you" (Ex. 20:12). It's the only one of the Ten Commandments with a promise attached to it. Perhaps God knew it would be one of the more difficult commands for some of us to obey. Adultery has never been a temptation for me, but back-talking my mother was all too easy, especially when my patience with her had worn thin.

Interestingly, the Hebrew word for "honor" is *kabed*. According to *Vine's Expository Dictionary of Old Testament Words,* one of its meanings is to be heavy or make weighty. When the command to honor our parents moves from respect and obedience when we're younger to determining how to best care for them when we all get older, it becomes a weighty command indeed.

How we honor our father and mother changes throughout the seasons of our life. Once we become parents ourselves, we experience this with greater insight. We expect our young children to be obedient and respectful. As they grow and mature, we hope for meaningful dialogue and moments of revelation where the rules and lessons we've taught them seep into the core of their hearts and we begin to glimpse the fruit of our labors in the form of godly young men and women. In our children's journey to manhood and womanhood, our parental role transforms from that of being the teacher to the role of a guide, and the respect and honor between us become even more mutual.

> HOW WE HONOR OUR FATHER AND MOTHER CHANGES THROUGHOUT THE SEASONS OF OUR LIFE.

That role reversal will happen with us and our children, and more immediately it will happen with us and our parents. Whether due to our parent's declining mental or physical state or both, we become the parent and caregiver and sometimes also the teacher and guide. Despite all these transitions, though, the need to honor remains the same.

In addition to this very specific command to honor our parents, the Bible often mentions how important it is to care for widows. This emphasis on widows is likely because then—as now—women tended to outlive men. I still think it's safe for us today to apply these principles and interpret these many verses as including both older women *and* men who are left with no spouse to care for them in a time of incapacitation or impending death.

When God was setting up Israel's governing system, he clearly provided for those who were in need—including widows. In Deuteronomy 14:28–29 he told the Israelites, "At the end of every three years, bring all the tithes of that year's produce and store it in your towns, so that the Levites (who have no allotment or inheritance of their own) and the aliens, the fatherless *and the widows* who live in your towns may come and eat and be satisfied, and so that the LORD your God may bless you in all the work of your hands."

Again we see that providing for those who can't provide for themselves has a promise attached: "that the LORD your God may bless you in all the work of your hands."

With the Israelites' tendency to throw feasts and parties, it's not hard to imagine that this once-every-three-year event was quite a celebration. I envision it not unlike our own Thanksgiving tradition of bringing together far-flung family and friends for good food; fellowship; and, later, football. This is just one example of many biblical mandates to care for widows.

WE'RE CALLED TO CARE FOR OUR PARENTS.

The New Testament gets even more specific about caring for parents. First Timothy 5:3–4 isn't just specific, it gets downright personal: "Give proper recognition to those widows who are really in need. But if a widow has children or grandchildren, these should learn first of all to put their religion into practice by caring for their own family and so repaying their parents and grandparents, for this is pleasing to God."

Wow. Put our religion into practice. Now we're getting too close for comfort. You mean my beliefs have to be borne out in my actions? We're called to care for our parents and grandparents as their mental, physical, and emotional needs increase with age. It's payback time, so to speak. Depending on the quality of our relationships with them, this task may be easy or hard, but it's nonetheless a biblical requirement.

This calling to care for our parents is consistent with the Bible's teaching. God's Word is all about relationships—from the first Old Testament relationship recorded between God and man in the garden to the New Testament relationships between Jesus and his followers. It's no wonder the Bible commands us to honor and care for those who brought us into the world.

Did you know there are more than seventy-three verses in the Bible using the phrase *one another*? By far the majority of these emphasize loving, caring, living in harmony, accepting, showing mercy and compassion, encouraging, honoring, serving, and being in fellowship. They're not about judging, teaching, condemning, or being too busy or active on committees. There's a lesson here.

While there is *stuff* to do, including the essential planning and preparation for end-of-life decisions and situations, the relationship-related exhortations are mostly just about that: *relationships*. Being there. Cultivating, building, and nurturing relationships.

When you've made your list, checked it twice, and realized your own family dynamics may not allow you to accomplish all that's required to plan for the future, fall back on the second greatest commandment, "Love one another."

All the planning and preparation and legal documents in the world can't take the place of genuine fellowship with one who's facing death. Behind the crusty, crotchety exterior is a dad who just wants to know his son really cares. Behind the controlling, stubborn woman who refuses to even talk about a will is a mom who longs for her daughter's love.

At the end of the day, our planning is about material, earthbound stuff. Sure it's our duty, responsibility, and obligation borne out of the demands of a complicated world run by rules and laws and forms filled out in triplicate. But it will all pass away eventually.

If you have read this chapter and felt overwhelmed by the to-dos and decisions, if you're considering the dynamics of your broken, blended, or blessed family and you are thinking, *We can never get all this done,* please take heart.

"Above all, love each other deeply, because love covers over a multitude of sins [and unfinished business and unresolved decisions]" (1 Peter 4:8). The myriad Scripture passages that encourage us to build relationships show us that in situations where much seems out of control, the most important thing is something we *can* control: how we care for one another and provide for both our own and our loved ones' hearts. It's that glimmer of hope that takes us into the next section of the book and allows me to share even more deeply how, by God's grace, I survived our family's slow dance at death's door.

PART THREE

Protecting the Heart

Above all else, guard your heart,
for it is the wellspring of life.
—Proverbs 4:23

PROTECTING THE HEART

It doesn't take great intellect or insight to realize we have to take care of ourselves to be able to take care of others. However, in the chaos, confusion, and pain that surround caring for our aging parents—often while working and raising a family at the same time—we feel the true weight of what's called the sandwich generation. Taking even a moment off seems unrealistic and selfish to the point of being unchristian.

In this section, I want to make the case for taking that time anyway. The Bible tells us to guard our hearts, for they are the wellspring of life (see Prov. 4:23). In spite of the increasing demands and pressures placed on us, we simply must take care of ourselves, guard our hearts, and allow ourselves the freedom to take much-needed breaks. In the end, we'll be much more able to gracefully endure the stresses and strains of caregiving.

So, in "My Personal Word," I'll share the practical strategies I used for getting through. I'll tell a few funny stories from the midst of the pain and discuss ways we can protect our hearts from the all-out assault we'll feel as we face our parents' end of life.

In "The Experts' Word," we'll read about the facts surrounding aging—the natural changes that occur as our folks face their final days. These will help us understand how to protect both our hearts and the hearts of our loved ones. We'll also hear what people who make a living dealing with the dying have to say about this all-important topic of caring for the caregiver.

Finally, we'll see in the Bible how God penetrates our lives with a beacon of light when it seems we're in impenetrable darkness. We'll see the scriptural justification for taking care of ourselves and letting him love us. We'll be reminded that he delights to meet us when we're weakest and most vulnerable. He's consumed with restoring our hearts when we're most distraught and heartbroken.

7

MY PERSONAL
WORD ON
PROTECTING

I mentioned before how hard it is to convey the extraordinary difficulty of this season of my life. Others have walked this path before and will in the future, and many of their situations will be even graver than mine. But at the time it was the worst thing I'd been through.

Others' stories are full of broken relationships and malpractice claims. There are distraught moms caring for dying parents and seriously ill children at the same time. There are men wrestling to provide for their own children while enduring a parent's sudden and unexpected death only days after their wives walk away from the marriage. There's the single woman, struggling with the loneliness of an empty apartment and an empty job, who finds herself dealing with a sick mother and seemingly useless siblings.

You can let your imagination run wild with stories of heartbreak and loss and fill a hundred seasons of reality TV shows and daytime soap operas. Whatever the scenario, it has probably happened.

With this cheery preface I open my own heart even further with the express purpose of demonstrating how much God wants to *protect* our hearts. It's essential to being an effective caregiver and sustaining our other relationships outside our caregiver role. Furthermore, it's essential to walk in the grace that only God can give during a time of unimaginable pain and grief.

I have four suggestions to help you protect your heart so you emerge from this season of life stronger and even more peaceful, albeit weary. I did these things—sometimes planned, sometimes not—but in retrospect they helped me get through this trying time. They're not necessarily listed in any order of priority or preference, and I encourage you to adapt my ideas to your situation and lifestyle. There's no right or wrong here—just do *something* to take care of your soul.

GOD WANTS

TO PROTECT

OUR HEARTS.

The first is to journal. Yes, men, you too. The second is to take time for yourself occasionally. The third is to spend time with your loved ones—the ones you're not taking care of, like your spouse, siblings, or best friends. The last is to remain conscious. I know that one sounds particularly crazy, but I'll explain it later. First, let's talk about the "Dear diary" stuff— and, guys, don't check out here. This isn't just a girl thing, and, besides no one will know. So hear me out and be open to how God can use this in your life.

⌖

Journaling became a lifesaver for me during my ordeal with my parents. I was pretty forthright and honest with my dearest friends about my frustrations and heartaches, but just between me and the paper I could write the most gut-wrenching thoughts with no fear of reprisal. I could dump my thoughts and feelings out between the pages of a decorated book and cry out to the Lord in prayers only he could read and understand. In any personal crisis, keeping a journal is a cheap form of therapy and a very effective way to stay in touch with your heart.

It's essential to walk in the grace that only God can give.

Here are a few entries so you can see what I mean. Note the dates; it will reinforce why I call this my slow dance at death's door:

Sunday, November 28, 1999

> *Mother seems to be the same in terms of behavior and forgetfulness. Maybe she's worse mentally; I don't know. She looks awful. Her face is puffy. Two of the fingers on her paralyzed arm are infected, and one nail is about to come off. I shudder to think what her toenails must look like. I was trying to doctor her and doing a terrible job. It was so natural and easy for Dee (my mother-in-law) to be compassionate and merciful toward her. Wayne kept saying, "Just try to see Jesus in your mom." Yeah, right.*

It's so hard to do that with someone so incredibly neurotic.

I've been wrestling with feeling like there's something I need to do before this will all be over with. I wrestle constantly with wanting her to get worse so it will be over soon.

Saturday, August 19, 2000

I've just begun a three-week family leave from work. Since I last wrote, Dad almost died from a morphine overdose and Mom is now bed/wheelchair bound with a broken leg and arm. The hospice doctor has confirmed cancer in her lungs, chest, bone, and brain. It's very slow moving, though, and up until now her body has been able to fight it off. Now that she's less mobile, it'll be tougher to fight, so things could speed up. Still no predictions on how long.

I can't control this. I can't make it happen faster. God forgive me for my selfishness in wanting her to die. I want my dad with me while he's still relatively healthy. God forgive me for my wretched selfishness. Let me confess it daily until it is gone.

Friday, June 1, 2001

Well, actually, it's after midnight, so I guess

it's technically Saturday. I'm up with a pounding, rapid heartbeat. I'm having stress-related tachycardia (racing heartbeat) like I haven't had in years. Too much worrying and not enough prayer. So instead of being on my knees before the Father I'm lying here fretting and figuring I'll die before my mom. I know I wrote yesterday "one day at a time," but I'm having a tough time doing that. It's so much easier to default to the "what ifs."

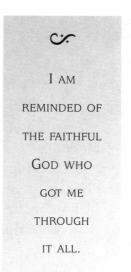

I AM REMINDED OF THE FAITHFUL GOD WHO GOT ME THROUGH IT ALL.

I told you I was brutally honest and heartfelt in my prayers. There were moments during my writing where I felt I was literally shaking my fist at heaven like David in so many psalms. Even now, it makes my teeth hurt to read my raging emotions and remember how often I fluctuated between somewhat selfless giving and pure, unadulterated selfishness.

The freeing thing, though, is to reflect back on how my heart was pulled through the fire. I'm able to see my toddler-like tantrums balanced by moments of sweet rest and peace. I am reminded of the faithful God who got me through it all, never once wincing at the rawness of my words.

Journaling helps us in another way too. When we're going through any kind of personal crisis, well-meaning people with pure intentions but faulty execution will say really stupid things to us.

Things like, "Oh, I know exactly how you feel."

Highly unlikely.

Or statements followed by questions like, "Well, it will

all be better when she's in heaven. Your mom *is* a Christian, isn't she?"

Well, duh. Intellectually I know this, but it doesn't mean my heart isn't breaking now—and who are you to question my family member's salvation?

Lauren Littauer Briggs wrote a great book titled *The Art of Helping: What to Say and Do When Someone Is Hurting*.[1] It provides wisdom and guidance to help us say the right things in difficult situations and includes many true-to-life examples to help us *really* help those who are hurting.

For those times, though, when someone hasn't read that immensely useful book, your journal can be a safe place to pour out the I-can't-believe-what-Aunt-Elbefern-said-today stories. We can smile kindly, say thanks, and convey to our trusty journal that people really don't understand what we're going through and that honestly we just wish they'd shut up.

WHATEVER IT IS THAT REFRESHES YOU, DO IT, AND DO IT AS OFTEN AS POSSIBLE.

Head to your local bookstore this week, get a cup of coffee, and buy a blank book. Splurge on a classic new pen, something that feels good in your hand and writes elegantly regardless of the quality of your handwriting. Don't write in your journal with the scratchy ballpoint with the missing cap you use to pay bills. Make the whole process something like a ritual, something sacred between you and God.

Put your crisp new journal with your Bible and make a date with both several times a week. The combination of reading God's Word and writing your own is a winner and one that helps your focus stay appropriately balanced between self versus others.

Wait a minute! Did I just imply that it's okay to focus on yourself? Even during a parental caregiving crisis? Yes, that's exactly what I implied. An occasional look in the mirror at your own soul is a critical strategy to help survive a season such as this.

The second tool in the toolbox for keeping your heart intact during family stress and crisis is taking time for yourself occasionally.

Good Christians are often plagued with the notion that we have to be focused on others 100 percent of the time, all the time. However, remember how often Jesus went out alone to pray and be with his Father? To gardens, the desert, the wilderness, the hills; he got away. He had alone time to refresh and renew his mind and heart so he could focus on his mission.

That kind of time alone is essential for us, too. (Remember, mothers, when your children were toddlers and you begged for someone to put *you* in time-out?) How we refresh depends on our personalities. Extroverted, life-of-the-party types get reenergized being with people. Invite them to festive gatherings and they leave ready to go to another one. The true introvert will relish a week alone in a cabin with no one to talk to but an occasional spider. Most of us are somewhere in between.

Whatever it is that refreshes you, do it, and do it as often as possible. If you're literally providing around-the-clock care for your terminally ill or incapacitated loved one, this is an all-the-more-important break. Check with your hospice provider, doctor, or local elder-care services agency for respite-care providers. These are trained and loving individuals who can come in and temporarily take over your duties so you can have a much-needed break. There are also adult day-care centers where Dad or Mom can spend the day with others from his or her generation while you shop, run errands, or go to a movie with friends.

While we were going through our family's trials and traumas, we owned an RV, a nifty home on wheels I could easily manage alone—and I took advantage of it. I'd load it up with my favorite dog, a few prepared meals, my laptop, piles of pictures, and the kids' scrapbooks. I'd head an hour or so out of town for a few days and work on writing projects and the chronicles of my children's lives. Somehow, taking the time to cut and paste pictures of their childhood helped me deal with the final demise of my own innocent and youthful years as I watched my parents dying.

If you have a zillion other family responsibilities, and most of us do, this getaway time may require calling in the troops. Remember all those conversations when the ladies in your Bible study said, "Oh, if there's ever anything we can do, let us know," or when a few friends at the office offered to cook meals for you or watch your kids? It's time to make the call. Moms, your husbands can manage with a bit of backup help. Line up a few after-school play dates, buy some frozen lasagna, and get out of Dodge.

Your escape doesn't have to be fancy or expensive. Find a local bed-and-breakfast. Even being five miles from your house can *feel* a million miles away. Explain your situation to the inn owner and you might even get a price break. It never hurts to ask.

Men, find an NBA or NFL game and go to it. Or rent a DVD of Wimbledon's greatest hits or golf's greatest bloopers. Whatever captivates your mind, take time to enjoy it. Tell your management team you'll be a much better employee after a day or two away and take your well-earned time off. Or hire a neighborhood kid to mow your lawn next weekend and zip away then.

Time away doesn't always have to involve leaving the county. I love my garden and backyard. I can easily spend a good hour back there just listening to the birds and meditating on God's creation (instead of the stack of medical bills for a change) and afterward I return to reality refreshed. For some, that same refreshment may come from wandering the quiet aisles of the library or the noisy bustle of the shopping center. Sometimes just seeing all that life and energy and watching the new moms on stroller patrol at the mall are enough to remind us that life goes on even when one life is ending.

WHEN IN
CRISIS, TAKE
PEACE AND
QUIET
WHEREVER
YOU CAN
FIND IT.

When I was still managing my parents' care from Austin and finding myself all too often at the hospital in Fort Worth, I discovered the hospital chapel. My aunt was the director of volunteers at this hospital for years. When she retired, the hospital administration looked for a way to honor her. Aunt Faith was a woman of grace, style—and deep faith. When it came time to remodel a wing of the hospital, Faith Chapel was dedicated. It was a very quiet and sacred space in the midst of buzzing machines, flourescent lights, and rushing professionals trying to solve some medical mystery.

More than once—while waiting for some test result or doctor to return a call—I wandered down to Faith Chapel to pray, rest, and bask in the quiet knowledge that God was really in control even though I didn't feel like it at the moment. Those times were made even more special by the knowledge that this holy space was dedicated to the memory of my precious aunt. When in crisis, take peace and quiet wherever you can find it. Sometimes it's just down the hall.

Most of us are great at coming up with excuses about why we can't possibly do this. We say we have too much to do, have to work, have a meeting next Thursday, a deadline on the tenth. Well, we need to apply that same excuse-making creativity to developing a plan to get away.

Oddly enough, some of the best time I had away wasn't just in the RV with my dog and my scrapbooks. After we moved my parents and they were comfortably settled in their new nest in Austin, I had to go back to Fort Worth and conduct an estate sale. Of course, plenty of family heirlooms and antiques came to Austin, but there was also a lot of bizarre stuff that had accumulated over forty-two years in the same house—a house that had an enormous attic and entirely too much storage space—all of it filled to the maximum.

My husband offered to come, too. A few friends offered to join me. But I felt it was something I needed to do alone. I didn't even take my dog, which for me is a big deal!

There was something very therapeutic and cathartic about throwing away the junk and trash and sorting through the family treasures and memories. It was a fitting parallel to what we all must mentally and emotionally go through as we face our parents' end days. I laughed. I cried. I cautiously wrapped up the bread-dough bowl and well-worn rolling pin. I carefully packed the family Bibles and Dad's Coast Guard uniform.

I watched with amusement the next day as devoted garage salers picked through the vases, ashtrays, dorky 1960s lamps, books, and odd assortment of stuff laid out for their shopping pleasure. They snatched up quirky things like wallpaper samples and sewing patterns from the '70s. As Mom used to say, people will buy anything.

It was downright weird to watch items from my childhood home walk out the front door. But at the same time, it was reassuring to see things in the hands of happy people who would enjoy them and give them new life.

Jeannie, one of my parents' first caregivers, had just moved into a new home. She bought quite a few pieces of furniture and my mother's old sewing machine. It warmed my heart to think someone who'd poured so much of her life into caring for my folks would provide a needed home for some of their possessions.

At that point I had lived in Austin for almost twenty years. I had my own meaningful belongings, my own household identity; my parents had all they needed in their new abode, and I was okay with letting a lot of it go. Others might make different choices. Each family is different and should choose how to handle family possessions individually. Some folks lock up the family home after Mom and Dad have moved out and don't open the doors until well after their parents have died. You have to decide what's right for your situation. And keep in mind as you work through these issues that I had the only-child advantage that many don't have. You may need to reach a compromise with several siblings or other family members.

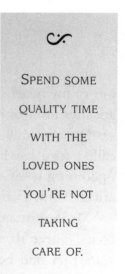

SPEND SOME QUALITY TIME WITH THE LOVED ONES YOU'RE NOT TAKING CARE OF.

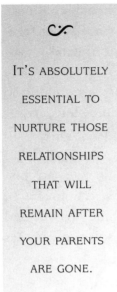

IT'S ABSOLUTELY

ESSENTIAL TO

NURTURE THOSE

RELATIONSHIPS

THAT WILL

REMAIN AFTER

YOUR PARENTS

ARE GONE.

After the estate sale and the cleanup, I checked into a comfortable hotel downtown, ordered room service, and took a hot bath. It was over. I'd finally spent the last night in the room I'd come home to thirty-nine years before, wrapped in receiving blankets and sporting pink booties.

Was it hard? Yes. Was it also refreshing in a way? Yes. For it was the closing of a chapter, the moving on to new things. It was a powerful time of reflection, hard work, and prayers for strength tossed heavenward while negotiating the price of an old computer desk. It was the time alone that I'd needed not only to get things done but also to clear some stuff out of my heart and mind. God used that time to bring me to another level of healing and peace.

On the way back to Austin the next day, my husband called to ask what kind of schedule I had at work for the upcoming week. It was near the holidays and things were relatively slow. I could get away. What did he have in mind?

Mr. Spontaneous had thrown together a trip for the two of us. Three days later, I was on a plane, sitting in first-class seats that had been procured with frequent-flier points, and headed toward a beach. The kids were happily in the care of grandparents. Even at their tender ages they sensed Mom and Dad needed to get away. This brings me to my third strategy—spending some quality time with the loved ones you're not taking care of. This may be your spouse, your best friends, or a beloved sibling.

We were fortunate; we had the flexibility and family support to do this more than once. But even if it's nothing more than a regular date night to the local diner and dollar movie, it's absolutely essential to nurture those relationships that will remain after your parents are gone.

When you're facing the intense care and nonstop decision making of elder-parent issues, being with someone who's willing to just love you and not demand anything for a few days is like manna from heaven.

My husband and I had another time away together that was oddly refreshing too. It was the weekend before the aforementioned estate sale, and we had headed to Fort Worth together to pack up more stuff and do some intense cleaning at my parents' home. My dad was thrilled that Wayne wanted all his tools and gadgets from his workshop and had given him instructions on where to find what and how to pack and store it.

My husband headed to the garage, and I made my way through the attic and kitchen cabinets. We were armed with boxes, garbage bags, and work gloves, and we scurried through the house like pack rats in reverse, reaching to the backs of drawers and shelves that hadn't seen daylight in years.

Like my experience with the estate sale, it was bittersweet—fun in a weird sort of way. You gain even more insight into the people you've known all your life when you see the stuff they've saved for years. My parents' survival of the Great Depression was obvious; they had saved everything and stocked up on stuff like pickles and cake mix.

At one point, I had my head in the back of a deep kitchen cabinet. I was pondering why anyone would need six pie plates when my husband appeared on the back porch. He'd

been in the garage for two hours and was covered with cob-
webs, dust bunnies, and dirt. He looked like Indiana Jones
returning from a dangerous expedition.

"Come out here. You won't believe what I found." He
was laughing, so I knew it wasn't the skeleton of some long-
lost relative. Lying in the driveway was an old, tattered
package. It looked like a twenty-pound bag of flour. In old-
fashioned letters it was marked *Acme Killin' Powder.* Yes,
Killin' with an apostrophe. And Acme just like in the old car-
toons. It was a sack of DDT, an insecticide banned in 1972
due to concerns about its effect on both the environment and
humans. It was buried on a garage shelf. My chemist mother
and her oddities! Try finding a hauling service willing to take
DDT off your hands.

Our three days were filled with interesting discoveries like
that: expired medicines, half-consumed boxes of crackers, and
stacks of catalogs and old magazines. Rotted blankets hiding
some of my old toys. Treasures among the trash. I was thrilled
to find a gold mine of old 35 mm slides, including pictures
I'd never seen of my grandparents.

Did we work like dogs? Yes. Was it tough and dirty and
gross? Yes. But it was a sweet time for my husband and me.
He got a new glimpse into my crazy family life. We spent our
evenings at some of my favorite old hometown restaurants.
We fell asleep exhausted and at peace over all that was being
accomplished and over the blessing of knowing my parents
were safe and sound in their new place in Austin.

Getting time away with your spouse, best friend, or perhaps brother or sister is crucial to your survival during this
season of life. Think of the times Jesus himself spent eating and
drinking with his disciples and local townsfolk, enjoying the
refreshment of good food, laughter, and fellowship. Don't

neglect the relationships that still will be with you once your parents are gone.

Before we moved my folks, I often had to make choices about whether to run up to Fort Worth for a weekend visit or stay in Austin for a ball game. As long as I knew there wasn't a crisis looming with Mom or Dad, I usually opted for spending time with my kids. I believed at the time, and still do, that under certain circumstances it was more important to invest time in my children who would be with me for many more years.

This is the reason we continued to go on family vacations and weekend camping trips even when things weren't well with my parents. My father was especially supportive of our trips. When we were wrestling with whether or not to go on a lengthy road trip, Dad was insistent: "You can fly home if you have to. Go. Don't sacrifice these memories with your kids."

Remember the advantage of respite care if you're a solo physical caregiver. Find out what services are available in your community. They're often available at significantly reduced fees or free.

As I mentioned earlier, some folks might try to make you feel guilty for such self-indulgence. "Well, I didn't leave your grandmother's side for six weeks," Great-aunt Mildred might say. Or, "What are you thinking, running off to Chicago for the weekend with your father in this state?" No one has walked in your shoes. Only you know what you can do with a clear conscience that will allow you to return with a renewed

> THE ULTIMATE GOAL—RENEWING YOUR HEART AND SOUL SO YOU CAN CARRY ON.

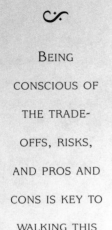

BEING CONSCIOUS OF THE TRADE-OFFS, RISKS, AND PROS AND CONS IS KEY TO WALKING THIS PATH IN PEACE.

heart. And this is the ultimate goal—renewing your heart and soul so you can carry on the task to which you've been appointed.

My final tactic for keeping your wits about you and your heart intact is—staying conscious. John Eldredge, in his book *Waking the Dead,*[2] makes the point that most of us don't live alert and awake to what we're thinking or feeling about what's going on in our lives, much less our heart condition.

When faced with a decision to go out of town, get away, or do something that might seem self-indulgent, I had to stop and think, *Am I okay with this? Will I feel guilty later?*

Am I okay with selling the LP record collection that's been gathering dust for twenty years—as long as I keep the 1938 78-rpm record featuring my great-uncle singing "On the Road to Mandalay"? Am I okay donating my mom's beautiful suits to the ladies hospital auxillary thrift shop so someone who needs them can use them—as long as I keep her antique, genuine-lizard handbag? It's all about choosing what's right for you and your family and situation. Choices range from the sublime to the ridiculous, but both impact the condition of our hearts and souls.

The decisions we'll face at this time aren't always about us. More often than not, they're about our parents and their care. At one point we made a decision to stop my father's cancer treatment. Because there was a suspicion that his prostate cancer might mestastacize and spread, he'd been taking a hormone treatment every few months. It made him miserable. He had hot flashes and night sweats, of all things, and it made his skin itchy and tingly.

We finally sat down with the doctor and had a long talk about quality of life versus treatment and came down on the side of quality of life. Dad was willing to perhaps sacrifice a few months in order to enjoy more fully the time he had. Besides, the cancer treatments were harder on his failing liver, and that was the disease that concerned us all much more anyway. We stopped the chemo treatments.

Those are always excruciating decisions. Second-guessing yourself and your doctors is easy. Being conscious of the trade-offs, risks, and pros and cons is key to walking this path in peace.

We faced similar decisions with my mother. Her cancer was spreading slowly in spite of continued chemotherapy. Her withered and useless arm caused constant pain. And in her increasing weakness she was constantly falling and breaking bones.

When you daily stand at the foot of a hospital bed and view the broken, bruised, and battered body of a woman who used to dig flower beds, clamber all over a boat, and conduct tours of local gardens, it's heartbreaking. You become intensely aware of the body's finite nature and our earthbound existence, and you begin to question the wisdom of prolonging life when it seems so pointless.

Heart-wrenching, gut-level decisions made with doctors, caregivers, and mentally shaky patients are devastating. These choices demand that we stay prayerfully connected to our heart, soul, and mind. We need objective, competent healthcare or hospice partners and open and honest communication with siblings to make wise choices we can all live with later.

When family dynamics prevent that communication and conversation from happening, we must guard our hearts or be saddled with guilt over situations in which we had no control. If guilt sneaks in, our hearts wither and grow cold.

My good friend Susan wrestles with this situation now. Her dying mother lives with Susan's sister on the other side of the country. Both the mom and sister deny the gravity of the stage-four lung cancer that has ravaged this woman. Only recently have they even agreed to let hospice come in and help manage the care of her increasingly weak and pain-racked body.

A thousand miles away, my dear friend Susan, a nurse, wrestles with being pushed out of the picture. She's heartbroken not knowing if her mother is getting the care she needs, and due to her profession, she's all too knowledgeable of her mom's medical condition and the pain relief available to her. In her heart of hearts she wants nothing more than to step in and take charge—or at least be more actively involved in this dire situation.

However, the family game hasn't dealt her a winning hand. More than forty years' worth of dysfunction is well entrenched, and a wall has been erected that she can't penetrate. So my friend has to guard her heart. She must manage the creeping guilt and keep it at bay, knowing that she can only do what she can do and nothing else. She can love her mom long distance, call and make sisterly suggestions, and fly out there whenever she can.

Her time with her mom is precious and her negotiations with her sister intense. But she learns to lean on God, who is in control over all things when we can't control any. She must lay her mom on his altar daily and pray for his divine intervention so her mother gets the care she needs.

And slowly, things change. As her mother weakens, her

sister relents and needs are met. Additional care is provided and Susan senses greater peace. She can only do this when she's conscious of her own heart and soul. By the time this book is printed, Susan's mother will be gone. Susan will be in some stage of managing the grief we all experience when we lose a parent. But by God's grace she'll enter the grieving process with the full consciousness of her heart. She'll have done what she could do and contributed where she could. At the end of the day, that's all any of us could really desire.

To recap, my four suggestions for protecting your heart are keeping a journal, taking time for yourself, spending time with loved ones, and remaining conscious of the condition of your heart. Leaning on God in this difficult journey and employing these strategies help us be better caregivers of both our parents and ourselves.

These suggestions are just that, though—suggestions. They're based solely on my experience. But what wisdom do elder-care experts and hospice workers offer about caring for the caregiver and surviving this season intact? Read on and find out.

---

1. Lauren Littauer Briggs, *The Art of Helping* (Colorado Springs: Life Journey/Cook Communications, 2003).

2. John Eldredge, *Waking the Dead: The Glory of a Heart Fully Alive* (Nashville: Thomas Nelson, 2003).

Helping ensure that our parents remain independent and active for as long as possible and frequently recognizing the accomplishments they've made and continue to make are critical in helping preserve the health of their hearts and core identity.

8

THE EXPERTS' WORD ON PROTECTING

ॐ

This section is really all about thriving through a season of chaos. Not just surviving, or getting through, but actually emerging at the other end of the tunnel stronger—even more peaceful—in spite of the inevitable pain and grief.

Not only can we protect our own hearts as we walk this path, but we can take steps to protect our aging parents' hearts too. As I reflect on my own experience, I recall now things we did that helped my parents through this process. I wish I could say our actions were all intentional. In reality, it was probably a combination of love, chance, and divine inspiration.

Now that I've studied a bit more about aging and the dying process, I realize the experts have a lot to say about the mental and emotional changes our parents go through as they approach their final years. They also enthusiastically support the notion that we must take care of ourselves in order to be in condition to care for our mom or dad. Highlighted here are a few of those facts and some practical advice that can help us view the sunset of Mom's and Dad's lives with joy and peace.

One of the most significant changes that psychologists and experts on aging will tell you about is how our identity changes as we age. Not only do our roles as children change—that role reversal we've already discussed—but deeper identity issues occur too.

During those reflective golden years, we're likely to look back on our lives to determine what we've accomplished and what we've contributed to our family, community, and society as a whole. Many elderly people struggle with the transition from productive member of society to what's perceived as less productive. The phrase that was knocked around for years was "becoming a burden to society."

Ageism—the discrimination against individuals based on age—used to be a significant problem in Western society in particular. There was a dramatic rise in the number of institutions where families could drop off Uncle Albert or Great-grandma Sue and let someone else worry about their care. How we dealt with old folks was very different from many other cultures where the aged were elevated in society's eyes and often even revered.

An unspoken assumption existed that old people were just in the way so someone else should deal with their care—care that was all too often messy, undignified, and difficult. After all, who wants to spend their days making pureed pot roast and changing really big diapers?

Unfortunately, there were too many cases of elder abuse

and neglect at poorly regulated nursing homes. Fortunately there was a collective outcry from the senior community and their adult children. As a result, the tide began to turn. Today, as more and more baby boomers enter their golden years, there are more choices for care, running the gamut from active senior retirement communities to invalid care at traditional nursing homes.

One of the most significant driving factors behind this shift isn't just the need for qualified, professional, physical care, but the recognition that the average seventy-plus senior isn't ready to be put out to pasture quite yet. The desire and need to remain active, productive, and contributing to society is a recognized and legitimate issue.

> THE DESIRE AND NEED TO REMAIN ACTIVE, PRODUCTIVE, AND CONTRIBUTING TO SOCIETY IS A RECOGNIZED AND LEGITIMATE ISSUE.

Helping ensure that our parents remain independent and active for as long as possible and frequently recognizing the accomplishments they've made and continue to make are critical in helping preserve the health of their hearts and core identities. This is even more important when their bodies begin to fail and they sense a greater loss of control over how they feel when they wake up every morning.

There was very little from his Fort Worth home that my dad insisted should come with him to Austin. Among the items he couldn't part with, though, was a model of the last airplane he'd worked on for Lockheed Martin and some paintings and illustrations done by his work buddies. They were reminders of his identity, his talent as a commercial artist.

My aunt's nursing-home room was the same. Every square inch of her walls was covered with her needlework—a remarkable skill she was known for among all her friends and family. Where there wasn't a bit of stitching, there were photographs of grandchildren and great-grandchildren—the apples of this sweet old lady's eye.

Allowing our parents to hang on to things that give them joy and remind them of who they are is critical to helping them through the aging process and the inevitable questioning of their identity and contributions to their family and community.

It's healthy for us, too. As we watch their list of physical ailments grow, reminding ourselves of their productive past and ways in which they still contribute to our family helps us remember that aging is a natural process.

Aging and elder-care experts also say one of the most important things to ensure the elderly's quality of life is to help them be independent as long as it's safe to do so. I've already mentioned some things that can help our folks stay on their own as long as possible. Sitters, nosy neighbors, and remote-calling devices such as Lifeline can help maintain normalcy for those who are reaching the tottery stage.

My paternal grandmother is a great example. Mamo lived alone until she was 101. She volunteered in a nearby hospital gift shop for so many years they lost track of her hours. She still baked pies and made the potato salad for family gatherings well into her late nineties. As I remember it, she was the one who finally put her apron down and told us she had retired from cooking.

My dad and his sisters lived close by and made sure she had plenty of meals; the next-door neighbor in the duplex kept an eye on her; and she wore a push-button pendant on a chain around her neck, so she could call for help if she fell. Dad built a ramp with a handrail so she didn't have to deal with stairs, and they took down the sliding-glass shower door and put up bathroom handrails so falls were less likely.

My grandmother remained an avid crossword puzzler and could still beat anyone who played her in Scrabble or rummy. She solved most of the puzzles on *Wheel of Fortune* before the contestants and read voraciously (both her Bible and sweet, old-fashioned romance novels). Mamo also had quite a collection of paint-by-numbers paintings on her walls. Encouraging these activities helped keep her mind sharp and active.

She was a remarkable woman with a will of iron, and fortunately her hotline to God kept her safe and sound in her little nest. Undoubtedly, one reason she lived as long as she did was because she was able to be in her own home for a long time. Not until she became very weak and began falling frequently did my dad and his sisters opt for a nursing home.

Mamo wasn't the least bit happy about this transition. As often happens, her health began to decline even faster once she was out of her little house and surrounded by more elderly and frail people. There were no other choices for our family though. Her children—all in their seventies—weren't in adequate shape to take care of her themselves.

In spite of the sadness of those last few months, the efforts made to keep her as independent as possible ensured that her final years were mostly very happy. Her identity was and always had been wrapped up in being a loving mother, grandmother, and great-grandmother—and that didn't change. In fact, it was reinforced as she approached the end. In spite of her failing body, her eyes lit up when we would visit, and she could often be heard humming her favorite hymns, long after her once-angelic voice had failed.

One final thing worth mentioning about the aging process and protecting the hearts of those we love is the natural process of slowing down. As we age, everything shifts into low gear. Our ability to process information begins to decline. You may have noticed this with Great-aunt Doris. She used to be the life of the family birthday parties, chatting up a storm with everyone and thoroughly enjoying the commotion from her favorite chair.

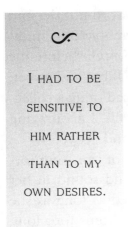

I HAD TO BE SENSITIVE TO HIM RATHER THAN TO MY OWN DESIRES.

Nowadays, though, family parties seem to overwhelm her. She misses too much even with hearing aids and can't distinguish one conversation from another. She tries to pay attention to the grandkids' stories, but more often than not her eyes glaze over and she seems a million miles away. This is both a normal and inevitable part of aging.

One of my dear friends experienced this recently with her remarkable one-hundred-year-old granny. For the first time ever, the family decided it was best for her not to attend the huge family Christmas gathering with all its noise and commotion. In her dementia and slower mental state, she'd reached the point where she didn't enjoy herself anymore. Instead, everyone took turns going to see her at her Alzheimer's residence. She was thrilled at the frequent visits over the holidays, and seeing her sweet family (some of whom she still recognized) in small batches helped preserve her dignity and heart.

I also saw this happen with my own father. There were times toward the end when we'd try with all our might to get him to join us on an outing. While his physical frailty was certainly a deciding factor—some days he just didn't feel like moving around—I could tell from his reserved behavior in noisy groups and new situations that the real reason he elected to stay in the quiet routine of his apartment was more because he felt overwhelmed by all the activity.

I had to be sensitive to him rather than to my own desires to get him out and about.

This is one of those clear examples of putting our elders' needs ahead of our own. While it might be heartbreaking to think of Grandpa not attending a festive family function, if he's happier in his own quiet nest, the family might be doing him a favor by letting him avoid a situation where he'll feel uncomfortable and unable to process all that's going on.

Social workers and those who deal often with the aging concur with the decision to carefully choose when and where Mom and Dad venture out. If there's a high-fall risk or a strep-throat epidemic among the kids in your family, then an outing to Uncle Jim's birthday party may not be a good idea.

> CAREFULLY CHOOSE WHEN AND WHERE MOM AND DAD VENTURE OUT.

Experts also agree on the notion of taking care of the caregivers. In fact, as we've mentioned, they can be the best resources for helping you figure out how to get time away to nurture your heart.

"I had a family member who used respite care once a week so she could go to the movies," Cathy Tuohy says. In the dark stillness of the movie theater, this worn-out daughter slept. "It was dark, no one bothered her, and the phone

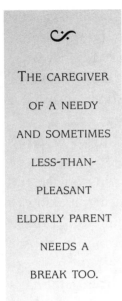

THE CAREGIVER OF A NEEDY AND SOMETIMES LESS-THAN-PLEASANT ELDERLY PARENT NEEDS A BREAK TOO.

didn't ring. It was the only place she felt like she could really get away while her mom was dying."

Hospice workers encourage creativity when it comes to getting some down-time. If you're caring for your family member in your own home, getting away is more difficult, but it can be done with the help of friends, other family members, and respite-care services. Use the agencies in your area to figure out your options. "If it's nothing more than an hour in the local coffee shop, then it's still better than staring at the same four walls, the laundry, and the bills that need to be paid," Tuohy says.

If your mom or dad is in a care facility, things may seem easier. But when you go home, there's still that pile of laundry, unpaid bills, and a lawn that needs to be mowed. Knocking a bucket of balls across the driving range or wandering through your favorite home-improvement store may be all the diversion you need. "Your time away doesn't have to be complicated," Tuohy says. The important thing is to get away.

I'll close this section with a few frightening statistics on elder abuse that reinforce the argument for caregivers to take care of themselves. According to the National Center on Elder Abuse, the number of elderly who are mistreated is appalling—and growing. Abuse can be physical, emotional, or pure neglect. What's worse, the abuse usually isn't at the hands of cruel or incompetent staff members of facilities or agencies. Ninety percent of the time, abuse is perpetrated by the person's own family members according to the 1998 *National Elder Abuse Incidence Study*.[1] The primary abusers are adult children.

Just like a new mom with a trying toddler needs time away to regain her sanity, the caregiver of a needy and sometimes less-than-pleasant elderly parent needs a break too. We can become overwhelmed by stress and pressure, and any of us at any time can succumb to the frustrations and aggravations brought on by caregiving.

Hopefully none of us would ever consider physical abuse of our parents—but then again, physical abuse is rarely premeditated. While I never reached this point, my sharp tongue got the best of me occasionally (with my mother especially), and in frustration I said hurtful and unkind words I later regretted.

Before the pressure cooker of this essential but seemingly endless role becomes too much and we say or do something we regret, we *must* plan for and take time to care for our hearts. Does the Bible offer any suggestions for this idea? Is there any kind of biblical mandate for what may seem selfish? Let's look.

---

1. The Administration on Aging and the Administration for Children and Families and the National Center on Elder Abuse at the American Public Human Services Association. *The National Elder Abuse Incidence Study.* Newark, Delaware: Clearinghouse on Abuse and Neglect of the Elderly, Department of Consumer Studies, University of Delaware, 1998.

In spite of the mounting pressures, in spite of the torment and guilt and enemies at our doorsteps, may our hearts live.

THE INSPIRED
WORD ON
PROTECTING

ᴄ·ᴧ

We've already mentioned Proverbs 4:23, the wisdom writer's call to guard our hearts above all else. Interestingly, this admonition is tucked in with verses about listening to instruction, gaining wisdom, avoiding bad company, and just generally behaving yourself. And what does King Solomon in his divine inspiration say? "Above all else"— more important than anything else I've mentioned here—"guard your heart." The Hebrew word for "guard," *natsar*, means to protect and maintain. Furthermore, the translation here for "heart" implies not just feelings, but will and intellect—broadly speaking, the center of everything. So the encouragement to guard our hearts involves a lot more than just recovering from our first broken heart or getting over a coworker's insulting words during last

IT MAKES
SENSE, REALLY,
THIS FOCUS ON
THE HEART.

week's staff meeting. And according to Solomon, it's even more important than behaving yourself!

It makes sense, really, this focus on the heart. After all, Jesus taught that the greatest commandment is to love the Lord our God with all our heart, soul, mind, and strength—and the second most important is to love our neighbor as ourselves. To love God with all our heart, we must take pretty good care of that center of everything—as the Hebrew word indicates the heart is.

Psalm 69 is one of the most frequently quoted psalms, and rightly so. It describes a roller coaster of emotions ranging from the depths of despair to the highest praises and hopes. Reading it, I'm reminded of my own heartfelt cries for help when the burden of watching my parents die was beyond what I could bear. Take a look at David's words, embellished with thoughts that could belong to any of us:

> Save me, O God, for the waters have come up to my neck. I sink in the miry depths [of decisions and paperwork and bills and my own family's pressures], where there is no foothold [or rest or peace or joy]. (vv. 1–2)

Sound vaguely familiar? How about verse three?

> I am worn out calling for help [and from talking to endless doctors and nurses]; my throat is

parched [and I have no time to sit and enjoy a cup of coffee or a glass of tea!].

It gets better, though. Verses 13–14 read:

> I pray to you, O LORD, in the time of your favor; in your great love, O God, answer me with your sure salvation [and your assurance that you're in control, because I'm sure not]. Rescue me from the mire [and my self-doubt, guilt, and frustration], don't let me sink [in the quicksand of the island of lost caregivers]; deliver me from those who hate me [and it seems Mom does half the time, in spite of all I'm doing for her].

We could go on with one lament after another. When we're in touch with our hearts—the core of our being—we sense both joy and pain intensely. However, there's hope at the end of this song. Look at verses 30–32:

> I will praise God's name in song and glorify him with thanksgiving. This will please the LORD more than an ox, more than a bull with its horns and hoofs [more than all the stuff I'm doing for everyone; it will please him when I stop and praise him in spite of my mood]. The poor [and the nurses, doctors, health aides, and insurance clerks] will see [my faith in spite of it all]

OUR HEARTS MEAN MUCH TO GOD.

and be glad—you who seek God, *may your
hearts live!*

There it is! *May your hearts live!* In spite of the mounting pressures, in spite of the torment and guilt and enemies
at our doorsteps, may our hearts live. Our hearts, where,
according to Ecclesiastes 3:11, God has set eternity. Our
hearts, which John 14:1 encourages us
not to allow to be troubled—our hearts
mean much to God. It's no wonder he
tells us to guard and protect them
through life's trials.

WE MUST
PROTECT OUR
HEARTS AND
THE HEARTS OF
OUR LOVED
ONES.

One of Jesus' most often-quoted
commands goes hand in hand with all the
verses regarding the importance and safe-
keeping of our hearts. In Mark 12:31,
we're encouraged to love our neighbor as
ourselves. While that doesn't imply that I
should install a shrine to myself on my
bedroom wall, it does infer that a healthy
bit of caring for myself is important if I'm
going to be able to love others—espe-
cially when those others are increasingly crotchety and
demanding old folks who often forget to say thank you. Yes,
love others as ourselves is a critical thing to remember. After
all, that verse is the core of the Golden Rule: Do unto others
as you'd like them to do unto you.

There's further evidence that time to nurture our hearts is
biblical. I mentioned how Jesus himself often went away to
pray and to be alone. In Luke 21:37, we're told that "each
day Jesus was teaching at the temple, and each evening he
went out to spend the night on the hill called the Mount of

Olives." We can safely assume that the Mount of Olives wasn't a bustling suburb filled with fast-food joints and entertainment venues, but rather a quiet place where Jesus could retreat from his hectic day and his intense time with the people who wanted so much of his attention. Sound like a familiar set of demands?

You must admit that if he—who claimed to be the Son of God and Creator of all things—needed to get away for a little rest, then an occasional break would probably be a good idea for us, too. While our role as caregiver does not call for anything as dramatic as turning water into wine or raising a little girl from the dead, our loads of decisions and responsibilities often seem to require a bit of miracle working.

As we enter into the roles of caregiver, decision maker, facilities manager, human-resources manager, financial manager, and all the other hats we must wear, we must protect our hearts and the hearts of our loved ones. It's essential. It's necessary. God commands it. Jesus models it. What more encouragement do we really need?

PART FOUR

*Preserving the Past
for the Future*

We owe it to ourselves and the generation that comes after us to learn as much as we can about those who came before us.

PRESERVING THE
PAST FOR THE
FUTURE

ℭ✶

Now before you jump into this section, let me encourage you not to view it as another to-do list. The process of chronicling and preserving our family's story is just that: a process. There may be ideas here that you choose to add to the things you are already doing with and for your parent or parents. There may also be things that you file away in the back of your mind for another, less stressful day.

The need is great though. As one generation passes from this life, a treasure trove of stories and hopes and dreams and adventures passes away with it. We owe it to ourselves and the generation that comes after us to learn as much as we can about those who came before us.

In that spirit, I offer you my own story of how I ultimately "preserved" my family's past. What started as simply cleaning out a bunch of old boxes turned into a history lesson with moments of giggles and times of tears. It is my hope that the ideas herein will inspire you, when the time is right, to consider how your family's story might be told.

Who knows, there might be a nonfiction best seller buried within Aunt Martha's tales of the years after the war, your dad's adventures building a business, or your mother's accomplishments in her home and city. You just never know … there is always a tale to be told.

10

My Personal
Word on
Preserving

As we neared the end with both my mother and father, I found myself suddenly asking lots of questions. When exactly did Betty meet Charlie? Where were you stationed in the navy, Dad? What was it like during the Great Depression, really? I recognized I was running out of runway and wouldn't have my parents around much longer. I needed to learn all I could about their lives while they could still remember their own stories.

Later, when the first waves of grief had worn off and I began meeting with counselors and social workers to learn more about dealing with this difficult season, I was hit by a blinding flash of the obvious. I woke up one morning, and God gave me an insight: What I had done was preserve the past for the future. There is an art, a science, and

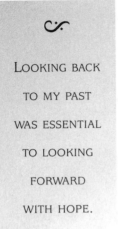

LOOKING BACK TO MY PAST WAS ESSENTIAL TO LOOKING FORWARD WITH HOPE.

logic behind doing this—and doing it purposefully.

I suddenly became aware of how the Lord used both sweet and bittersweet memories and tales from my family's history to make the end of a generation more bearable. I realized looking back to my past was essential to looking forward with hope. I became convinced that understanding our family's legacy is a crucial step in letting go of those who have moved on and the raising up of a future generation.

In my personal experience, there was something about reviewing not just my parents' lives but my life as well that brought a broader perspective and different angle to the trying stage I was going through. I found myself digging through boxes and carefully turning the weathered pages of our ancient family Bibles to glean what secrets I could about my family tree and the faith and failures hidden there.

It all started with those 35 mm slides I mentioned previously. When we were cleaning out my parents' home, I found the box of slides. Now, I knew my mother saved everything so my expectations weren't high. I figured they were of some garden show or civic event that she and my dad had been asked to preserve on film—or worse, boring photos of obscure computer parts from my dad the illustrator's moonlighting projects. What I found, though, was the all-out mother lode of family lore and legend.

Standing unwarped and straight as soldiers in their trays and boxes were surprisingly old slides of my mother as a young woman, years before she'd met my father. There were pictures of her with my grandparents in California, Colorado, and New Mexico, enjoying the sights and picking up souvenirs and rocks (of all things) in forests and desert landscapes that had seen tourists of all shapes and sizes traipse their paths for generations.

Now believe it or not, those rocks are significant. Mom had always told me that those chunky pieces of petrified wood that rested on my grandmother's porch had come from the petrified forests of California. (That bit of scavenging had probably occurred long before it was a federal offense to take anything other than oxygen out of a national forest.) Those pieces made their way back to Gram's hometown in Texas and rested at her subsequent houses among bits of amethyst and quartz and a conch shell of mysterious origin.

The rocks—which now rest on *my* porch in Austin—have now come full circle. It is the rocks that remind me to tell a new generation the stories of travel and family memories and adventures and what it must have been like to travel Route 66 long before the song was written, stories that tell of the importance of both making and preserving family memories and histories.

Suddenly, sitting on the floor of my parents' old bedroom, flipping through hundreds of slides and tossing aside the ones of landscapes with no people, I saw my mom and her parents in a new light. Stories of my grandfather suddenly take on deeper meaning. The claim that my grandparents never got along is diminished by a photo of them dancing in the living room of their farm, grinning from ear to ear and obviously dolled up for a night on the town. The living room in the background is furnished with a love seat and rocking chair that now rest in my own home. And believe it or not, draped across my grandmother's arm is a delicately beaded handbag from the 1930s that hangs in my hallway.

There were photos of a great big Chrysler sedan and men in felt hats and ladies in gloves and suits, because that's how you traveled when you were well bred—or were at least trying to act like it. There were shots of my mother with her father standing on the deck of some ship—probably in San Diego Harbor. Their eyes were glittering, showing hints of a love that can only exist between a daughter and her daddy and giving me insight into the pain Mom must have endured when he tragically ended his own life in 1954.

Beyond the insight into my mother's premarried life, there was a treasure trove of photographs from the pre-Amy days of my parents' marriage. There were pictures from their wedding anniversary in Mexico and subsequent trips they'd made to the sunny country south of our border. Mom had become something of a self-educated expert on Mexican art and culture. Her photographs of Taxco and Acapulco were spectacular, and I remember her coming to my third-grade class to narrate a slide show and to tell stories of her Mexican adventures. Her favorite was of Mexican glassblowers asking her for her spent flashbulbs. (Remember flashbulbs?)

I'd seen the slides of Mexican cathedrals and artisans making pottery and serapes. I'd seen the photos of the Mayan ruins and beautiful beaches. The pictures I'd never seen, though, were what caught my eye and heart. They were newlywed-era scenes of Mom and Dad on their balcony, playing cards and enjoying the view of crystal blue waters and tropical trees. A photo of a toucan happily perched on the back of a balcony chair. Pictures of my dad riding a donkey across a stream on some schmaltzy tour, his size 13 feet dragging in the water. I'd heard the story all my life. It was part

of my family lore, but I'd never seen the
photo. There it was in my hand.

The discovery of those slides awak-
ened a desire to capture my past—more
specifically, my family's past. Each of us is
part of a larger story—a story filled with
both the heartwarming and heartbreaking. Each family is saddled both with
stellar stories and skeletons in the closet.
Understanding these and chronicling

EACH OF US

IS PART OF A

LARGER STORY.

them are a huge piece of teaching our children and other generations to come to our faith and hope in the future.

This process started with the newfound discoveries of my
parents' past but moved quickly to my own short but adven-
turous journey through life. I mentioned earlier my tendency
to journal. Long before I started writing, I was cutting and
pasting. One of my cousins had turned me on to scrapbooking long before there were scrapbooking contests,
magazines, and classes and three aisles in the craft store
devoted to the endeavor.

I had scrapbooks dating back to about sixth grade. They
were ridiculous (and I'm sad to admit, falling apart from—
ugh—*age*). Every birthday card I'd ever received is there.
Every spirit ribbon from every football game and basketball
game during my middle- and high-school years. Ticket stubs,
family's and friends' photos, and postcards from others' journeys. I criticized my mother for hanging on to everything that
couldn't crawl away, but I wasn't much better.

One weekend I set aside time to sort through it all. I figured at that point, after over a decade of marriage to the same
man, it didn't make a lot of sense to keep cards and love notes
from my high-school sweetheart. So I culled through those

and other things that were beyond meaning to me any longer and kept only those things that would really tell my life's story. I created two albums that started with photos of my family home surrounded with three inches of snow the day I was born and progressed all the way through my early years of marriage.

> ℃⁓
>
> I SAW THAT THERE WAS MORE GOOD IN MY CHILDHOOD THAN I'D OFTEN CHOSEN TO REMEMBER. THE WHOLE PROCESS WAS A REMINDER OF GOD'S GRACIOUS PROVISION FOR ME.

It's the Amy Croxton Baker story. It's likely that no one but me will ever really care. Oh, I'm sure someday my kids will get a kick out of it and appreciate the time I took to tell my life's story in picture and word. But it was a cathartic experience for me and one I took seriously as I considered someday passing my family's legacy of faith and life adventure to the next generation.

While caring for these two people who at times were driving me nuts, it was very therapeutic to look back on the memories of our lives and sort through the good and the bad. It wasn't unlike throwing away the junk in my family home and saving the antiques and heirlooms that spoke of our more precious past. During the process of tearing and clipping and cutting and gluing, I saw that there was more good in my childhood than I'd often chosen to remember. The whole process was a reminder of God's gracious provision for me.

In most areas of my life—marriage, work, friendships, and

children—I'd chosen to look at the glass as half full instead of half empty. But there were definitely times I'd looked at my own past and childhood as though the glass was not only half empty but cracked, too. The photos, the cards, the letters, and the bits of nostalgia reminded me of all the good things my parents had done for me over the years.

It set in motion the next step I took to chronicle our family's story. When I cleaned out my parents' house, I not only found all the photographs my mom had taken; I found other interesting odds and ends, too. My dad's navy yearbook—which he'd illustrated, by the way. My mom's freshman-year (1944) grade report from the University of Texas, which was *quite enlightening* (I now claim a genetic disposition for my tendency to do poorly in math).

Beyond the photos were letters, licenses, identification badges, Sunday school attendance awards, and employment applications that told the stories of my parents' lives. There were awards and newspaper clippings of births and deaths and civic achievements. I set out to create a starting-at-birth album to tell Betty's and Charlie's stories. It was another of those weekend-away projects filled with scissors, glue, and felt-tip pens.

Please know these aren't award-worthy albums. There are no multiple layers of textured papers and stamps and ribbons and fancy cutouts. These volumes are purely functional. High-quality, conservation-worthy papers and binders, yes—but the Creative Memories crowd would be embarrassed by my efforts. It was more about capturing a past generation's memories so future generations could more clearly understand our family's story of faith and failing, struggle and success.

I mentioned earlier the importance of remembering a

person's contributions to family, community, and society, especially as they reach those frail years where it seems they contribute nothing. It was fascinating to me to find the photo of my dad when he was selected Employee of the Year at Stripling's Department Store in Fort Worth, some time after he returned from the navy. There he was, handsome as all get-out, with a paintbrush clenched between his teeth, preparing a show card for the department-store window.

I ENCOURAGE YOU TO EXPLORE YOUR PAST.

I also found an article from the *Fort Worth Star Telegram* dated 1944. It was about my mother winning awards from the Austin Camera Club for her color photography. The headline read, "Betty Wallace of Fort Worth Reaches for Fame with Color Photography." An interesting discovery considering my own career success would also begin in Austin.

These artifacts completed the circle. They showed me my parents as real people with real lives, not just as sick old people who had become dependent on me for most of their needs. They showed glimpses of faith and service to church and community, values that set the stage for how I'd be raised and how I'd raise my own kids and choose to serve and be involved in my own town years later.

Whatever this season of your life looks like, I encourage you to explore your past. Ask questions and make note of the answers while you can. Whether you do it in the middle of the chaos, as I did, or after it's all over with and you're dealing with your grief, make that leap backward and explore your family's history.

In *Mr. Sammler's Planet*[1] Saul Bellow wrote, "Everybody needs his memories. They keep the wolf of insignificance from the door." Recording our families' memories helps us see the significant roles we each play in God's grand design for humanity. From generation to generation we're all part of a great plan that's connected from beginning to end—from Genesis to Revelation, if you will.

This past fall my aunt died. Olive June was my dad's sister, her parents' firstborn. She was a stately woman—six feet tall. She never liked being called the *older* sister or *bigger* sister, so she humorously referred to herself as the *other* sister. She was my last remaining immediate relative from that generation. I have some first and even a few second and third cousins I keep in touch with, and they know some of the family stories, but their trees head off into different branches than mine. With Auntie Olive's passing, the original sources of the 1920s era and before in the Croxton family came to an end.

The remaining questions I have now about our family are lost with a generation that's gone. Sure, it's kind of amusing to think that our forty- and fifty-something crowd is in charge now. We finally get to sit in the nice dining room and make the little cousins clean the kitchen. But the curiosities and inquiries about our family that remain will now have to wait until I'm on the other side of heaven. When I finally get there, those questions will probably be the first I ask God (after I ask what he was thinking when he created the ostrich). Still, I've documented quite a lot. When my children ask me questions, I have decent answers—and that's a good feeling, both for me and for them.

Preserving the past for the future is really about showing our children they're part of a larger story of faith and glory, failure and redemption, history and hope.

All family stories look different. Your family history may be marked with devastating heartbreak and rampant, unrepented sin. Some of our relatives may have made choices that seemed to curse generations to come. But the power of forgiveness that God offers transcends generations. Our family's past may add shades of light and darkness and depth to our own lives, but it doesn't have to color it with doubt, failure, and condemnation. Remember, he who came to set the captives free and release prisoners from darkness easily breaks those generational curses.

If your family story is too dark to tell, then tell the story of God's amazing grace instead. Psychologists and social-service experts agree this is an important process in dealing with this final stage of our parents' lives.

---

1. Saul Bellow, *Mr. Sammler's Planet* (New York: Penguin Classics, 1970).

11

THE EXPERTS'
WORD ON
PRESERVING

J ayne Gaddy put it most simply: "Become your family's historian. Capture your family's legacy. There aren't many people who don't like to talk about themselves!" When she thought her mother was going to succumb to cancer, Gaddy went to her hospital room with a video camera and said, "Tell me everything." Fortunately, her mother beat back the cancer, but the exercise convinced Gaddy, who counsels mostly women and girls, that the effort to record a family's history is essential.

Gaddy also encourages clients to think about what she calls a life imprint. "Reflect on features about yourself that you've gotten from your parents: their mannerisms, activities, personalities, and values." In the all-important exercise of caring for our hearts, this lets us either cling to those imprints or reject them for more healthy ones.

THE KEY IS TO SIFT THE WHEAT FROM THE CHAFF WITHIN OUR FAMILY'S LEGACIES.

All of us observe characteristics in our parents that we don't want to imitate and behaviors or attitudes that we don't want to seep into our own hearts. I caught myself (and still do) saying things, then thinking, *I sound just like my mother!* Sometimes that's a good thing; sometimes it isn't. The key to keeping our hearts, souls, and minds intact during (and after) this season of intense caregiving is to sift the wheat from the chaff—the good from the bad—within our family's legacies.

Kids' school projects sometimes require them to interview an older family member or record some bit of family history for posterity and then write about it. It's another way to obtain family lore and legacy. Keep this stuff. Your child's English teacher may just be looking for a new angle to get kids to write, but the information gleaned will be meaningful to generations to come.

Even now, my husband's family is frantically searching through closets and bureau drawers trying to find the cassette tape that a cousin, Jen, made of Grandfather telling stories from the Battle of the Bulge. There's a piece of history on that tape Jen made for a senior project—not just American history, but family history, priceless memories that give insight not only to who their relatives were, but also to who they are.

For a graduate counseling class my husband had to create a *genogram*. This is a form of family tree that doesn't just indicate names, birth dates, marriages, and births, but *vocations*.

What had his ancestors done for a living? It was a fascinating study revealing that most of his relatives were self-employed craftsmen or tradesmen.

It makes sense as he's a self-employed craftsman himself now, helping hurting families restore their lives and marriages to wholeness with the help of God's amazing love. Psychologists recognize how heritage impacts our life choices. For students destined for the mental-health-services field, especially those planning to become marriage and family therapists, the exercise showed clearly how our past shapes our future and, consequently, our relationships.

I found it very interesting that as my dad lay dying—literally taking his last breaths—the hospice nurse who'd been at our side for the final few weeks asked me to tell her stories about my father. She'd been assigned to our case rather late in the game and hadn't gotten to know much about him. As I began to tell stories about my father—his life as an illustrator, community volunteer, and avid supporter of all my endeavors—I felt immediately stronger.

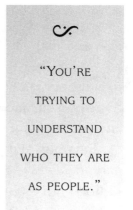

"YOU'RE TRYING TO UNDERSTAND WHO THEY ARE AS PEOPLE."

I was still aware of my sweet, dying daddy, but the question posed by this health-care professional—who'd witnessed who knows how many lives ending—made me both reflective and forward thinking. My dad had lived a rich, full life. He had accomplished much and was now on the steps of heaven. Sitting there, watching his chest rise and fall more slowly with each breath, I was able to tell her about the kind, talented, and strong man who had been my dad.

Several counselors I talked to emphasized a similar process when I asked them about tactics to help us understand and appreciate our family of origin. Rick Reynolds, the social worker and therapist I mentioned earlier, gives clients a set of questions to ask their parents. Some are downright personal, but if you can go there with your parents, it's worth it.

> "WHEN THE TRUTH BEGINS TO POUR OUT, IT REPLACES THE SOMETIMES ERRONEOUS MYTHS."

"You're trying to understand who they are as people, not just as your parents," Reynolds says. It's a sometimes difficult—but rewarding—experience when the insights and answers begin to fall like summer rain. "When the truth begins to pour out, it replaces the sometimes erroneous myths that may have revolved around our parents for years," he explains. We may decide some of those stories are best left unrecorded, but they still give us insight as to why our parents parented us the way they did. Stories of tragedy, pain, and disappointment shine a light on who they are and why they functioned as they did.

Reynolds suggests breaking questions into eras of your parents' lives. "Ask about their earliest memories through junior-high school—what is their earliest memory, for instance?" What was school like? Who was their favorite teacher? Progress from there to their thoughts on their own parents' marriage. Then move on to junior high through their wedding day. It's all part of legacy building.

This whole process makes facing the end of our parents' lives and our role in that much easier. This exercise of preserving the past for the future helps us face our loss with an expanded perspective on the people who shaped us into who we are—but it's also definitely about telling generations to come the stories of our family and its heritage.

God commanded the Israelites to retell old stories and understand where they came from as well. In his infinite wisdom he set in motion the chronicles of faith written by divinely inspired human hands to tell the story of his involvement in humanity from the beginning of time. Let's explore now the biblical examples that encourage us to preserve our past for the future. This preservation of the past isn't just something I came up with while I was surrounded by dusty boxes and ancient photographs. It isn't just a clever idea from the hospice, counseling, and mental-health community; it's a biblical principle worth noting.

> ‿
>
> PRESERVING THE PAST IS ABOUT TELLING GENERATIONS TO COME THE STORIES OF OUR FAMILY AND ITS HERITAGE.

One generation will commend your works to another; they will tell of your mighty acts.
—Psalm 145:4

THE INSPIRED WORD ON PRESERVING

The Psalms are filled with exhortations to proclaim God's works among all generations. Psalm 145:3–7 says,

> Great is the LORD and most worthy of praise; his greatness no one can fathom. One generation will commend your works to another; they will tell of your mighty acts. They will speak of the glorious splendor of your majesty, and I will meditate on your wonderful works. They will tell of the power of your awesome works, and I will proclaim your great deeds. They will celebrate your abundant goodness and joyfully sing of your righteousness.

This call to proclaim God's works from one generation to

another is just one of several passages where praising God goes hand in hand with history and generational stories. It's interesting to note the pronouns: "They will tell ... I will praise." It reminds me of sitting at my grandmother's feet long ago, listening to her tell stories of faith and hope during the Great Depression. They had very little, but they had each other and God and they were happy. She'd talk, and I'd sit in rapt fascination of her stories from a time when there were no phones and no electric lights and there was a celebration when the technology of the streetcar came to our town.

> "ONE GENERATION WILL COMMEND YOUR WORKS TO ANOTHER."

As you read in my family portrait in the earliest chapter, my home life wasn't perfect. I didn't grow up with daily family devotionals and the outright discipleship we strive to do with our children today. But there was definitely an undercurrent of faith. There was a legacy of involvement in church and a recognition that God was at work in our lives.

Your experience may be something much different. Your story may not be a song of praise but rather one of searching and a journey to faith. Perhaps you're the first member of your family to profess faith in *anything*. Perhaps you're still trying to figure out all this Christianity stuff. There are still good words for you to record—there's still a story to tell, even if it is just the story of your family's search for significance in its pursuit of success or struggle for sanity. Whatever your family's history, the story God weaves throughout your story is one of redemption and restoration.

If you think you had it bad, consider the Israelites. I daresay there's little in our sordid world that didn't occur in their culture as well. Their history is certainly filled with triumph and tragedy. The Old Testament frequently refers to curses passed down from one generation to the other—usually due to sin and disobedience. In spite of that, there's no disputing God's tireless pursuit of his people. There's no doubt of his love for them as he rescued them over and over again from their enemies and made a way for them to reach him through his detailed commandments and sacrifices.

In fact, some of his strongest words to them speak to this need to pass down stories from one generation to another. Look at Deuteronomy 11:18–21:

> Fix these words of mine in your hearts and minds; tie them as symbols on your hands and bind them on your foreheads. Teach them to your children, talking about them when you sit at home and when you walk along the road, when you lie down and when you get up. Write them on the doorframes of your houses and on your gates, so that your days and the days of your children may be many in the land that the LORD swore to give your forefathers, as many as the days that the heavens are above the earth.

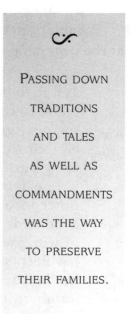

PASSING DOWN

TRADITIONS

AND TALES

AS WELL AS

COMMANDMENTS

WAS THE WAY

TO PRESERVE

THEIR FAMILIES.

Surely as the Israelite parents sat down to teach their children all that the Lord had commanded them, they were quick to tell the story of their remarkable escape from Egypt. In a culture of oral traditions and few written words, you can just envision mothers and grandmothers sitting by the fire with eyes glittering as they told their children not just the laws to be obeyed, but also the miraculous stories of the Red Sea parting and of munching manna from heaven every morning.

The Israelites saw their share of suffering, persecution, and setback, but their history—as recorded in the Old Testament—indicates they knew the power of storytelling. Certainly not all of the stories were ones of joy and jubilation, but they knew that passing down traditions and tales as well as commandments to be obeyed from generation to generation was the way to preserve their families and their position as God's chosen people.

Again, if you think your family story is too sad to tell, look at the beginning of the book of Joel, which says:

> Tell it to your children, and let your children
> tell it to their children, and their children to
> the next generation. What the locust swarm
> has left the great locusts have eaten; what
> the great locusts have left the young locusts
> have eaten; what the young locusts have left
> other locusts have eaten. Wake up, you
> drunkards, and weep! Wail, all you drinkers
> of wine; wail because of the new wine, for it
> has been snatched from your lips. A nation
> has invaded my land, powerful and without
> number; it has the teeth of a lion, the fangs
> of a lioness. (vv. 3–6)

It pretty much goes downhill from there. No, this wasn't a people who always had a pretty story to tell, but they chronicled their heritage anyway and knew the value of passing those stories down.

Jesus also used countless stories to convey his truths to the multitudes that came to listen to him teach. He knew the power of illustrations and oral traditions. Those stories gave rise to the New Testament church and our faith as we know it today.

There's a story in the Gospels worth our consideration. It shows how the powerful and poignant stories that reveal our inmost hearts can last forever. The setting is a meal at the home of a man in Bethany named Simon. A woman comes to Jesus while he's reclining at the table and proceeds to anoint his feet with expensive oil, the kind you'd pay a fortune for at the cosmetics counter at Saks Fifth Avenue.

It's a strikingly beautiful picture of devotion. Apparently, in her heart of hearts, Mary—unlike many others—understood the Lord's words when he foretold his upcoming crucifixion and burial. This jar of oil was worth a great deal of money in the Judean economy; in fact, it might have even represented this young woman's dowry. But she was willing to sacrifice it to anoint her Lord. Little did she know there would be no time for such ceremony when his broken body was gently taken from the cross. Nor did she have any inkling that when the other women returned to his tomb three days later with spices, there would be no body to honor with the Jewish burial traditions.

What a story! It's so significant it's included in two of the four gospels (see Matt. 26:6–13 and Mark 14:3–9). Listen carefully to Jesus' words about this event. The disciples are griping and grousing about the waste of this expensive oil when Jesus scolds them. In Matthew's account we see how strongly he felt. "Aware of this [their grumbling], Jesus said

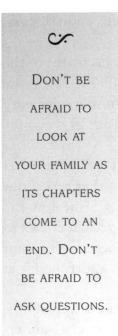

DON'T BE AFRAID TO LOOK AT YOUR FAMILY AS ITS CHAPTERS COME TO AN END. DON'T BE AFRAID TO ASK QUESTIONS.

to them, 'Why are you bothering this woman? She has done a beautiful thing to me. The poor you will always have with you, but you will not always have me. When she poured this perfume on my body, she did it to prepare me for burial. *I tell you the truth, wherever this gospel is preached throughout the world, what she has done will also be told, in memory of her'"* (vv. 10–13).

Wow! What she has done will be told throughout the world in memory of her. Here we are, two thousand years later, still repeating this story. One can only imagine the tales her relatives told about her for generations to come. *"Mary!? Yes, she was the one who anointed the Lord Jesus before he was crucified! Her love and devotion and faith in him were so pure! Oh, how the Lord loved and honored her."*

Friends, he loves and honors us, too. The power of his story intermingles with the story of our life and our family's past and present to create tales of beginnings and endings, stories of mishaps and mistakes, legends of restoration and freedom. Don't be afraid to look at your family as its chapters come to an end. Don't be afraid to ask questions, record the answers, and marvel at your life's story. It is written in part by your parents and the roles they played, but even more significantly, it is written by God's hand:

> For you created my inmost being; you knit me together in my mother's womb. I praise you

because I am fearfully and wonderfully made;
your works are wonderful, I know that full well.
My frame was not hidden from you when I was
made in the secret place. When I was woven
together in the depths of the earth, your eyes
saw my unformed body. All the days ordained
for me were written in your book before one of
them came to be. (Ps. 139:13–16)

Even by broken bodies succumbing to disease; even in the fluorescent-glow halls of nursing homes, hospitals, and dimly lit bedrooms, God shows up and takes his people home.

13

PIERCING THE DARKNESS OF DEATH

We're at the end now. The preparation of heart and soul is completed; the planning is done as well as it could be, so now we wait. As I close out the story of my family's slow dance at death's door, I want to tell you the story of their final hours, marked by that remarkable mix of pain, grief, and relief that can only be experienced as dark death comes to call and eternal life takes over to bring light.

Two things stand out in my mind when I recall this final stage. First, many hospice workers told me that how you are in life is how you are in death. In fact, those personality traits and character tendencies are often magnified. The chipper, happy-go-lucky types will be smiling to the end. Sad, bitter, and angry people will become even more so. The quiet will become quieter and the bossy, bossier. This was definitely my experience leading up to this point.

The second thing I heard over and over again is that dying is work. For the believer this makes sense on some level. We're passing from one life to the next, trading in our earthly trappings for something eternal and impossible to describe. Countless stories of near-death experiences—with their sightings of angelic beings and long-gone relatives—testify to this truth. However, I wasn't prepared for what I'd see as my parents themselves made this final journey.

> WE'RE TRADING IN OUR EARTHLY TRAPPINGS FOR SOMETHING ETERNAL.

All of us have days that are permanently etched in our memory, such as when the space shuttle *Challenger* exploded during the launch. The dreams of families and the hearts of Christa McAuliffe's students sinking into the Atlantic waters. I remember hearing on the radio that President Reagan had been shot, and standing there at work as a young college woman trying to make sense of such a horrible crime. I had no category for that kind of national tragedy.

Most recent, of course, are the unforgettable events of 9/11. So much has been written about that earth-shattering, life-altering day, I can't compose any new words.

Our memory embeds certain events in our hearts and souls, so that no number of years gone by, no amount of life's distractions can ever take them away. For me, the days my parents died created those kinds of indelible memories.

I don't tell you these stories to bring a tear to your eye but to light beacons of hope. Even by broken bodies succumbing to disease; even in the fluorescent-glow halls of nursing homes, hospitals, and dimly lit bedrooms, God shows up and takes his people home.

MISS BETTY

ᴄᵛ

It was a typical summer in Austin—hot and muggy. The kids had been playing with friends, swimming a lot, and enjoying our lax summer TV-watching rules. I was thinking about Mom. She'd looked really bad all week.

After she fell and broke her collarbone on May 26, there was no choice but to take her from the hospital to a nursing home. She simply couldn't go back to the assisted-living facility. Even with full-time sitters and extra care, she'd reached a point that seemed to be leading to the end.

> ᴄᵛ
>
> OUR MEMORY
> EMBEDS
> CERTAIN EVENTS
> IN OUR HEARTS
> AND SOULS.

Frankly, I was also beginning for the first time to worry about finances. Remembering that her mom had survived for years beyond anyone's expectation, writing checks with so many digits each month was beginning to make me nervous. Interestingly, Dad was fine with the idea of her not coming home to the place they'd lived together for nine months of their forty-nine years.

Of course I was skeptical about the whole situation. There had been so many bounce backs from what seemed to be the edge of death that part of me expected her to recover and demand to know where all her nice clothes and dress shoes had gone.

The most logical decision seemed to be the rehabilitative wing of a nursing home a few blocks from my dad's place. It would be easy to take him over there daily to see her. Oddly enough, Mom had few questions and no complaints about where she was going. We moved her TV and photos and introduced her to the "physical terrorists" who would be helping her get a bit more mobile again, and she settled quietly into a new routine.

THE "QUIETLY" WAS WHAT CAUGHT MY ATTENTION.

The "quietly" was what caught my attention. The woman who'd hollered at more than a few nurses and sent several aides running out the door in tears was uncharacteristically subdued. Her moments of alertness and lucidity were being replaced with hours of silent sleep and occasional muttering about someone long gone or asking questions that made no sense, even with my vivid imagination.

Here's an entry from my journal around that time:

> *I want to take it one day at a time but struggle with wanting this to be "it." It's difficult to not wish this ordeal over. She's so broken, bruised, and miserable. I don't think she has any fight in her. This is the longest she's gone without eating. I guess it's been five days without a significant meal.*

It wasn't long before it became completely apparent she had no fight left. She shunned the idea of any type of physical therapy, in spite of the handsome PT guys and charming young women who tried to bribe her any way they could to get her to exercise and move her wounded body.

Finally the kindhearted director of the facility called me. "We need to move your mom, Amy." It seems there are all sorts of rules behind which beds are used for what kinds of patients (Medicare-related rules that I don't pretend to understand), and they needed her room for someone who was ready to do the hard work of rehabilitation. We rolled her bed down the hall to a wing for the truly bedbound.

Those are the scenes from nursing homes that break our hearts—the diapered and waiting to die, some without families to come visit and few smiles to brighten their days. Fortunately, Mom was in a room by herself, and I only had to endure the sight of her failing body; no one else's.

By this point she was rarely communicative. Occasionally we'd get her to eat a milkshake or a meal-replacement drink. She didn't even ask for her daily diet soda anymore. No TV. No chatting. She had begun the descent toward death.

July 12, 2001, dawned like any other Texas summer day. Puffy, high clouds offered little relief from the heat, and the cicadas sang their man-it's-hot-out-here song from the trees. The kids were playing with friends, and my husband was out of town on a road trip with his father to visit some uncles.

That Monday, Mom had looked perfectly awful. I thought we must be nearing the end, but this time the hospice nurse was skeptical. "We'll see," said she who had attended so many deaths. "She's surprised us many times before." By day's end, though, Mom was even worse. Very labored breathing, that telltale rattle in her chest.

I called the hospice. "Can you just come take a look at her and tell me what you think?" I left to check on my kids and my dad, and an hour or so later my cell phone chirped. It was the hospice nurse. We'd been through so much together; she didn't even have to identify herself on the phone. I recognized her number on caller ID and her voice.

"This could really be the end, Amy, " she said. Mom's respiration was the telling sign. With each hour, it seemed to slow even more, and the death rattle became more pronounced. She wasn't in any pain, though, and didn't seem to be struggling to breathe in spite of the ominous sounds from her lungs.

I sighed. A mixture of resolve, relief, and unbelief filled my heart and I went to see my dad. He was finishing up lunch with his buddies, and I think they were having a heated discussion about baseball.

"Dad, I think we need to go see Mom. The nurses think this is it. She's really going to go soon." He was incredulous. "You're kidding," he muttered. That strange sense of relief must have pervaded his heart too. It was midafternoon by the time we made the three-block trip to the nursing home.

Indeed, she seemed to be taking her final breaths. She was completely unresponsive. I watched in dismay as the aide came in to change her diaper. It must be the ultimate loss of dignity, yet she didn't notice or seem to care. We sat there a while in silence; then Dad spoke. "Well, I think I need to go back to my place."

Everyone handles death differently. Dad didn't want to be there for the very end. I think that, at some level, she was

SHE WAS SO IN NEED OF HER HEAVENLY GARMENTS.

already gone in his mind. The social workers had always said, "Do what you know you'll be comfortable with later." He didn't want to be there, and I didn't press the issue. After all, he was tired and tottery himself, struggling with a failing body of his own and the weight of his eighty-one years.

I took him home and got him settled in for the evening in his comfortable and familiar nest. His buddies were happy to see him and offered their concerns and prayers for the situation down the street. I ran home to make sure my kids were happy spending the night with some dear friends, grabbed my Bible and a book, and headed back to the nursing home.

If even her oldest, dearest friends had wandered into the room, they wouldn't have recognized her. I was even stunned by her appearance in those final days—she looked like a just-hatched baby bird—hairless from the chemotherapy, sunken eyes, sharp features, and limbs contorted from brokenness and paralysis. She was so in need of her heavenly garments of glory and wholeness.

IT WAS AS THOUGH SHE WERE SEEING SOMEONE SHE HADN'T SEEN FOR A VERY LONG TIME.

In spite of her unresponsiveness, I talked to her. I figured, for once she couldn't argue with me. I reminded her I loved her and was glad she'd been my mom. I knew I wouldn't be the woman I was if she hadn't raised me.

I assured her of God's love for her and read from a book of prayers for the dying. I read the Bible to her: stories of new life and redeemed hearts and broken bodies made whole.

As I watched her labored breathing, I looked at her face and realized to my amazement that her awful frown lines were gone. The crevasses that had traveled down from the corners of her mouth for years had disappeared. Even more astounding, in these final hours, her facial expressions were constantly changing. She'd smile. She'd raise her eyebrows in surprise. It was as though she were seeing someone she hadn't seen for a very long time.

As the experts had told me, dying is work, and she was very clearly doing the work. It was remarkable to watch. There I was in North Austin, getting a glimpse into heaven on my worn-out mom's face.

My mother's journey had been a hard and very long one. She had fought death for years. Whether she wasn't ready to go or God wasn't ready for her, no one can be quite sure. Perhaps it was a bit of both. One thing was certain now, though. A difficult passage that had begun with pain, bitterness, anger, and resentment was ending with a relaxed countenance, peace, and contentment.

GOD WAS TELLING ME THAT HE HAD HER NOW.

In those quiet early morning hours of July 12, 2001, a lifetime of memories was spinning through my mind—laughter and tears and silliness and sadness. Summer trips and school projects and prom and graduation and a wedding. A spontaneous food fight in the kitchen that left us both covered in seven-minute frosting. She'd been through all of it with me, and although her demonstration of it wasn't always perfect, I never doubted her love.

Memories must have been flooding her soul, too, and in God's grace they must have been happy ones. The smiles were more frequent now, and her mouth moved in silence—perhaps greeting someone I couldn't see.

Now, don't get me wrong—I don't believe in praying to dead ancestors, but in the rapid-fire prayers that were going on in my heart, I was asking my aunt and grandmothers to tell her to come on. *"C'mon over, Betty. It's gonna be just fine."*

I sat there for a few hours, reading and praying, coming to a whole new understanding of the prayers the Bible calls "groanings too deep for words." A little after midnight I decided to go home, let the dogs out, and maybe lie down for a bit. I figured, knowing my mother, this wasn't going to be a quick departure, and she'd find something to get hung up on between earth and heaven. She'd probably get into some discussion with some saint at the legendary pearly gates, and this process wouldn't necessarily be over with soon.

About five that morning one of the dogs needed attention, so I shoved him outside and got back in bed. I decided to wait another hour to call and check on Mother. After all we had been through, I half expected to hear, "She's rallied! She's eating breakfast and demanding the newspaper!"

Back in bed, I drifted between wakefulness and sleep and had a vision—or maybe a dream. I really don't know what it was, but the message was clear. God was telling me that he had her now. What I saw in my mind's eye—not spookily hovering over my bed or anything—was my mom dressed in white, with long gray hair. She was smiling.

Not long after, the phone rang. "Mrs. Baker, this is hospice. I'm sorry to tell you that your mom has passed away. It's over."

Even after all we'd been through, even as ready as I was, I was still in shock. And then the mysterious grieving process took a backseat and my action orientation took over. It was time to start making calls. It was time to go get my dad.

He was awake and getting dressed by the time I got there. He greeted me with his typical joviality but quickly sensed the end had come. I really don't think he quite knew how to react. We went to the nursing home to say good-bye. There lay my mother, quiet and still, just looking like she was asleep. No more pain, no more anxiety, just peaceful sleep. It really was over.

Later that day—after the initial round of phone calls had been made—when the wheels were turning to take care of obituaries and memorial services and countless other details, I slowed down for a moment of reflection.

Suddenly my dream or vision or whatever you call it came to mind. At the moment she'd passed through heaven's gates, I'd seen Mother at peace. God had given me that serene view. It was blessed assurance that her battle had ended in peace.

Although her faith never quite looked like mine, although we disagreed on meaningless bits of theology and social issues, now we were both victors. My mother had her garments of white and was free from that which wreaked havoc on us all for years. I had the peace of knowing that all my prayers were answered for her to be at rest.

God is a God of grace and wonder, and it's no wonder he'd want my mom in heaven. Although she's finally peaceful, I'm sure she's still very busy and probably helping straighten out some eternal committee that only *she* is qualified to lead.

SIR CHARLES

The story of my father's final days is no less heart wrenching; it's just not as drawn out. Amazingly, after my mother died, he found a new lust for life. The woman he'd been married to for almost fifty years was gone, but in the end of her suffering and pain he found a new spark of energy and peace he hadn't known for years.

It may seem sad to think of a five-decade marriage ending and the surviving spouse being happier, but it wasn't happiness of a gleeful sort, just relief that the suffering was over. Relief that he could enjoy his remaining days with his daughter, son-in-law, and grandchildren with no worries in the back of his mind.

We had lots of fun in the ensuing months. He was getting weaker daily, more unstable and forgetful, but he was very happy. He thoroughly enjoyed his friends at the assisted-living facility, and there was that wonderful spur-of-the-moment trip with us to Hawaii.

He even went on a dinner date with a charming lady who'd had her eye on him for quite a while. Alas, he didn't know quite what to do with that. Some things never change. When it comes to relationships, the guys are often clueless!

Dad had stumbled and fallen a few times, scaring all of us to death as we remembered the broken hip the year before, but there was never more damage than a few bruises or tears in that paper-thin skin. Things changed, though, when my phone rang one February morning.

"Amy, your dad's fallen and we think he broke his arm. He's in a lot of pain and we've called for the mobile X-ray to come check him out." I whipped the car around and headed to his place, forgetting all about whatever else I thought I had to do that seemed so important.

Sure enough, the X-rays confirmed that his arthritic shoulder—the one that gave him fits of pain already—was shattered in several places. He was bruised from head to toe and looked like he'd been on the losing end of a street fight. The medical team was concerned about blood clots forming from the fracture. Did you know broken bones actually bleed? I didn't either.

We were facing another set of treatment decisions. He certainly couldn't withstand any kind of surgery even if it would really fix anything. His liver function had so affected the rest of his body that he'd never fully heal. I couldn't see dragging him to another set of doctors to be told, "He's in bad shape. Big risk of a blood clot here. That could kill him instantly if it hits his brain."

Well, to this frightened and worn-out daughter, that prognosis sure sounded better than the potential dementia and eventual coma that so often accompanied dying from liver disease. The thought of my father dying from some instant event was much more palatable than thinking that he might reach a point where he didn't recognize me for days or weeks on end.

So, we plodded forward from there. Lots of pain medication. Peaceful but much less chipper conversations and fewer requests for his favorites: cheeseburgers and chocolate malts. Visits from the grandchildren who left with puzzled looks on their faces. "Pop doesn't look so good, Mom."

His arm was in a hard-to-manage sling, and he was having a great deal of difficulty getting around. The bleeding from the break and his body's efforts to try to heal the mess in his shoulder left him weaker by the day.

March 2, 2003, brings to mind one of the worst moments of my life—one forever etched in my memory. I walked in his room to find my regal and dignified father lying on the floor, covered in urine and excrement, and bleeding profusely from his shattered arm. I was terrified and furious all at the same time.

The facility staff was horrified. My husband had visited Dad earlier in the day and Dad was holding his own. His favorite aide had checked on him moments before the fall, and he was okay, sitting up in his chair and dozing. Apparently, though, he'd tried to get up, and his body just collapsed. He really hadn't been crumpled there for long, but it was long enough to make everyone feel miserable.

Here's an entry from my journal that night:

> He'd tell stories and ask about life, sometimes trailing off into a world I didn't know.

> *Dad was hallucinating earlier in the day when Wayne went to see him. He occasionally didn't even seem to know his own son-in-law. When I finally left tonight around seven, he was talking like he was in the hospital. I think he thinks he's back in Fort Worth.*
>
> *It's up there with one of the worst experiences of my life and exactly what I've prayed we would avoid: the loss of dignity, the confusion, the total dependence on others.*

We brought in a full-time sitter to keep an eye on him. Alicia called him "Daddy" and doted on him like he was her own father. She quietly sat in the corner reading her Bible and flew out of that chair the minute he needed anything. The three of us would sit and watch TV together when Dad was awake, and he'd tell stories and ask about life, sometimes trailing off into a world I didn't know, making me wonder if we were nearing the end.

For a brief time, we considered bringing him to our home. We'd built a guest room specifically for that purpose with wide doors and room to accommodate a wheelchair and any other medical equipment he might need. When we really thought about it, though, we realized the noise and hustle and bustle of our rambunctious, kid-filled home (we called it Party Central) wouldn't be pleasant for him. Besides, he wouldn't have the company and visits from his dining buddies, who after nearly two years had become his fast friends.

> ∾
>
> I WAS
>
> WORN OUT,
>
> EXHAUSTED,
>
> AND
>
> DESPERATELY
>
> NEEDED A
>
> DISTRACTION.

The following weeks were tenuous. Occasionally he'd call me Olive or Faith, thinking I was one of his sisters. His blood pressure was fluctuating wildly, and more and more of our conversations made little sense, at least to me. The hospice team kept experimenting with different kinds of pain relievers to try and keep him comfortable without making him totally goofy and unintelligible.

By early April, he was alternating between being lucid and completely lethargic. At this point, we weren't even trying to get him out of bed because it hurt his shoulder too much to move him. He didn't seem to notice he was catheterized now, and his appetite—which hadn't been anything to get excited about for years—was pitiful now.

By late April, I'd reached the end of my rope. I was worn

out, exhausted, and desperately needed a distraction. I had to get away for a day or two.

I talked to my social worker about the seeming insanity of actually leaving town with my dad in the shape he was in. Again, I heard her wise question, "Would you be okay if he died while you were gone?" Yes. I would. "Then do what you know you'll be okay with to take care of yourself."

In the preceding weeks, my father and I had said both silent and verbal "good-byes" and "I love yous," and more than once I'd assured him, "Dad, I'm going to be okay." My father was as comfortable as he could be, was receiving excellent care, and was out of it most of the time. When he did wake up during my visits, some-times he seemed glad to see me, but most of the time he just slept.

WHEN GOD IS

IN THE

PICTURE, IT'S

PASSING

ON TO

A NEW LIFE.

So again, I loaded up the dog, my lap-top, and the RV and headed a short forty miles outside of town. Even today, tears fill my eyes as I read this journal entry:

Saturday, April 26, 2003, Pedernales Falls State Park

Just Valentine [the Labrador] and me. And a bunch of gnats.

My daddy is dying. I don't think he will hang on more than a week or two. I've been very depressed and sad about it, but I think I'm as ready as I will ever be now.

Easter was weird. At that point he and I hadn't had a conversation that made much sense in weeks. I already felt separated from him and suspected that sometimes he didn't know me. It was as if I had this infinitesimal glance of what Jesus and his heavenly Father felt at the prospect of the crucifixion—the first time they'd be separated in all of time. And to think he did that voluntarily for me.

ᴄ͡ʀ

THE REUNIONS

WILL BE SWEET.

During those few days away alone, and then back home in my twice-daily-run-to-see-Dad routine, I reflected a lot on resurrection and eternity, life ending and life beginning. It struck me that in spite of our calling it "passing away," that's not what it is at all. For when God is in the picture, it's passing *on* to a new life. Away, yes, from our earthly trappings, but passing on to something much better where there's no more sorrow, no more tears.

One day I realized in awe that soon my father would be reunited not only with his wife, but also with his mother and father and generations before from our family of faith. His younger sister, the one he saved from drowning in Lake Worth during their childhood, that sister who'd endured her own brave fight with death, would soon see her darling "big bruddah."

Even more fascinating to me was the thought that, somewhere in heaven, my father had a son. Not that his daughter hadn't brought him plenty of joy, but he also a boy he'd finally get to see. Dad would get to meet that son, a baby rarely spoken of, stillborn a month before his due date, two years before I was born.

Oh, who knows what heaven will look like? The Bible is pretty vague about it, but one definitely gets the impression it's going to be really, really good. The reunions will be sweet, the glory as thick and comforting as a slab of grandmother's best chocolate cake. (And with no calories even! I'm certain!)

All I knew as I entered that first week of May was that spring was abounding all around me and that hope eternal was in my heart. I knew with confidence I'd see my parents again. I knew we were nearing the end for my dad, but that end would mark the beginning of a new season for us both.

May 12 was the day. It was partly cloudy and not too hot yet. I'd had a 6:30 a.m. speaking engagement at a local church workshop, so I was up and out the door by six fifteen. I almost canceled—there was just something gnawing at my gut—but the show must go on, so I went anyway.

After I got through my presentation, I decided to brave the morning rush-hour traffic and go on out to my dad's. When I walked in the door, I immediately knew today was different. Alicia was leaning over my father, talking to him in muted tones and stroking his forehead. He seemed to be asleep, but his breathing was very rapid and painfully labored.

I looked at the dear sitter and she shook her head as we exchanged glances of concern and sadness. I practically ran down the hall to the nursing director's office. She stood as I entered and said, "I was about to call you. It'll be today, Amy. It'll be today."

I'm one of the strongest people I know. I can get through anything and juggle ten hats at once, but at that moment, my knees weakened, my heart fell to my shoes, and I thought I was going to faint.

"Okay, okay, okay. It's going to be okay," I said, trying to convince myself more than anyone else. "But isn't there something we can do to help calm down his breathing? He just looks like he's in pain." I was desperate for something to ease this transition that was so apparent now.

The hospice nurse arrived soon after and all concurred that an extra dose of morphine was the right choice. This is palliative care at its finest. Immediately, my dad began to relax. I talked to him and told him I was there and said, "I love you."

He mouthed those precious words back, his once-strong baritone voice unable now to make any sound.

I called my husband. Between gulps for air, I told him he better get here immediately after school if he wanted to say good-bye. Wayne appeared forty minutes later, not waiting for his final class to end.

My husband said later he thought he was prepared, but he wasn't. The sight of my sweet daddy, his beloved father-in-law, taking what would be his final breaths was beyond what he could bear. He sobbed silently as he held my dad's hand and said, "I love you, Charlie. It's gonna be okay."

It was then that the nurse asked me to tell her about my dad. "What did he do, Amy? He was an artist, right?" Indeed, illustrations by him and his talented cronies filled the room. As I sat in the chair a few feet from his bed and squeaked out a few stories from Dad's happy past, I didn't take my eyes off him.

He was quite still now. Very peaceful. Smiling and moving his mouth, just like my mom had, perhaps already singing with the other Croxtons in the heavenly choirs. I could see his chest rise and fall ever so faintly, and his jaw moved, too, as he took those last breaths, little puffs of air that did little but remind us of man's mortality.

And then the chest stopped rising. Midsentence in some

story, I rushed to his bedside. "Cathy, what's happening? His chest isn't moving but his chin is. What's going on?" She took her stethoscope and confirmed what I already knew. My heart was beating out of my chest, but his had stopped.

The kind nurse, who'd stood silently by and watched as so many had reached this moment, tenderly reached up and touched my father's chin. The involuntary movement stopped.

He was gone.

I crumpled into my husband's arms and sobbed. The roller-coaster ride of watching my loved ones die, four in a row counting my grandmother and aunt, had now come to an end. They were tears of grief of course, but tears of relief, too. They go hand in hand down your face, erasing all traces of composure while washing out the gunk that's accumulated in your heart.

My family's slow dance with death, blessedly saturated with God's gracious peace, was over.

> "Where, O death, is your victory? Where, O
> death, is your sting?" The sting of death is sin,
> and the power of sin is the law. But thanks be
> to God! He gives us the victory through our
> Lord Jesus Christ. (1 Cor. 15:55–57)

EPILOGUE:
PRAISING A LIFE
WELL LIVED

Honoring the memory of a loved one is a challenge. How many of us have sat through funerals, perhaps of an old friend or parent of a childhood buddy, listening to the minister wax eloquent about the dearly departed's accomplishments and characteristics and thought to ourselves, "Who is he talking about? Am I at the right funeral?!"

As I planned my parents' memorial services, I was fortunate. I knew their lives' accomplishments were well regarded and well respected, even if half of the people who'd known my mom were a little scared of her!

My desire wasn't only to honor them, but to give glory to the God who'd gotten me through hell and back during the past five years. As was their wish, we held memorial services in Fort Worth at the church where they had been married in 1952.

When my mother died, the pastor emeritus who had officiated at their wedding was still in good enough health to speak at her service. When my father died, the choir of which we'd both been members sang a soaring anthem proclaiming, "For God so loved the world ..."

Both moments were beautiful pictures of a family's long-standing legacy in a congregation. Those who came to pay their respects to my parents were old-time friends and family, some of whom I didn't recognize, a few friendships even dating back before Mother and Dad were married.

I'd paid tribute to my grandmother when she passed away a few years before, so I had experience with this eulogy thing. After all, I was a public speaker, used to addressing crowds from ten to thousands. I never doubted I'd stand before the assembled crowd to praise my parents' lives and give God the glory for our final years together.

It was, however, more difficult than I expected.

We chose to have my mother's service in the chapel. It was smaller and would provide a more intimate setting. So many of her garden-club friends had either passed away or were in poor health themselves that we really didn't expect more than fifty to seventy-five attendees.

After the first hymn had been sung, the first prayer spoken, I stood from my seat in the front pew and approached the lectern. When I turned and saw the standing-room-only crowd, my knees started to shake and my voice followed. By prayer, God's power, and watching my kids grinning at me from their spot by their dad, I got through it.

During the reception, there were fond memories and grateful acknowledgments of the life my mother had lived, what she had contributed to the community, and the legacy she had left through my family and me.

One woman, a member of our church for years, told me of the trees growing in her backyard. "You remember, your mother did the children's message every Arbor Day and gave saplings to all the little children in the service. Well, those trees are five and six feet tall today!" Life goes on in all its various forms.

You couldn't call it a crowd of *mourners,* because everyone knew how long my mother had suffered. It was, however, both a gathering of history and a glimpse of the future, children mingling with octogenarians, all having come to hear these words I spoke about my mom:

> *We're here today not to mourn a loss, but to honor the life and legacy of Betty Croxton. In remembering my mother with you, I want to reflect on several things: her legacy, her life's lessons for me, and how I've grown in my faith during the past years' journey toward her life's end.*
>
> *But first, there are some thank-yous. I'm grateful to our dear friends from Austin who risked life and limb on Interstate Highway 35 to journey here to be with us. Their prayers and support over the past years of my mother's illness have been remarkable. You all have truly modeled what the community of believers is supposed to be by bearing one another's burdens.*
>
> *Many of you here in Fort Worth have also continued to show your love and support with phone calls and cards. We were also blessed with some remarkable caregivers both in Fort Worth and Austin—people who showed tremendous compassion and kindness to a sick old lady who wasn't*

always the most pleasant patient. Some of you are here today. Please know how much we appreciate your gifts of mercy and support.

Finally, my father deserves the greatest recognition of all. For in spite of his own aging and health concerns, he has modeled devotion and loyalty in a marriage that's rare today. He has faithfully upheld the vow "in sickness and in health" during the past few years. If standing ovations were appropriate during a memorial service, you'd receive one.

Now from Sir Charles to Miss Betty:

My mother leaves behind a cultural district's gardens that are some of the most beautiful in the country. I learned more about Japan than I ever cared to as she developed the docent program for the Japanese gardens. Our patio was often covered with paper lanterns and umbrellas in preparation for some festival or event. The garden festivals she helped orchestrate not only encouraged weekend gardeners to cultivate beauty, they provided opportunities for me as well—I somehow found myself selling advertising for the program and the Redbud, *the Garden Club newsletter. Her work with the conservatory program was probably the most intense and most fruitful, as she and the-little-old-ladies-in-tennis-shoes helped raise millions of dollars to build the beautiful structure that so many now enjoy.*

"FROM MY
MOTHER'S MANY
PURSUITS I
LEARNED
PERSEVERANCE."

From my mother's many pursuits I learned perseverance. To never give up. To set a goal and achieve it. And, since she was so busy, I also learned to be a much better housekeeper than she was. She taught me to be a lady, how to set a table, and how to behave at a country club. She taught me how to cook and sew and polish grandmother's silver. She insisted I hold my head high when I was taller than all the boys and be proud of my Croxton height. She taught me how to bait a hook and clean a fish—something I have no desire to do now. She taught me to appreciate music—at the theater, at the symphony, and through seven horrible years of piano lessons. As a tribute to her, and because I finally want to learn to play, I start lessons again in September. She encouraged the gift of my voice, scrimping to buy my Castleberry High School Choir wardrobe and helping make costumes for musicals, not to mention chauffeuring me to countless rehearsals, whether at school or church.

She taught me the importance of my education and made sure I had good friends to hang out with by getting me to youth group, even if it meant driving from Eagle Mountain Lake to Ridglea Presbyterian every Sunday afternoon. And she shook her head in disbelief as I trekked out on my first backpacking trip to the New Mexican wilderness to pursue God in the mountains. She was supportive yet

"I HAVE AGAIN AND AGAIN BEEN REMINDED THAT GOD IS IN CONTROL."

didn't understand how a child from her loins could possibly want to pack the bare necessities on her back and sleep in a tent for five days. It's no coincidence that the faith that has carried me to this point today and given me the strength to stand here at this moment began upstairs in a youth room full of beanbag chairs and green-and-yellow shag carpet.

> ❧
>
> "I BELIEVE MORE THAN EVER NOW IN THE POWER OF THE HOLY SPIRIT."

Betty Croxton was a fighter. She fought city hall; she fought the park board; she fought the highway developers. She fought with whoever got in the way of whatever she was doing. And in 1985, she began her fight with cancer. Determined to beat it, she drove herself to chemotherapy and never got sick. She took her treatments, got a wig, and kept on going. But when the cancer resurfaced several years ago, her ability to fight was waning. Her arm was paralyzed—the result of a mistake in surgery. She only got to hold her newborn granddaughter one time. At that point, the feisty Betty we all knew began to die a little bit every day.

Fight she did against death itself, though. In spite of numerous pronouncements that this was it and we were close to the end, she seemed like a cat with nine lives and rallied over and over again. I believe in her heart she was fighting with God. Either she wasn't ready for him, or he wasn't ready for her.

The lessons I learned watching a parent die, a

little bit a day, for more than five years, were pro-
found. Another personality trait I believe I
inherited from my mother is a tendency toward
control. I try to call it the spiritual gift of admin-
istration, but it's really about me trying to run
my own life and be in charge. But this was a situ-
ation I could do nothing about. Through the long
and painful process of my mother's death and my
father's physical trials, too, I have again and
again been reminded that God is in control, his
timing is perfect, and he allows everything to hap-
pen for a reason.

Jesus said, "My grace is sufficient for you, for
my power is made perfect in weakness." I don't
like weakness. I'm just about the most competent
person you'll ever meet. I can rise to any chal-
lenge. I can create the image of having it all
together and seem to be a corporate leader and
June Cleaver all wrapped into one. But in the
past few years, my faith has been tested to its lim-
its; my heart, soul, and body have been their
weakest; and I've learned that my sufficiency is
in Christ and nothing else. When my faith was
lowest and my pain was greatest from watching
the woman who raised me suffer so, that's when I
felt God's presence most strongly, and that's when
something would happen to remind me of his per-
fect timing and his plan for our lives.

My mother was a fighter. She fought death for
a long time. She wrestled it. She was mad at it.
She was frustrated with it. And the whole ordeal
was very painful to watch. But there were prayers
being offered up for her for peace and to bring
quiet to her soul. I believe more than ever now in

the power of the Holy Spirit—that he will inter-
cede for us with groanings too deep for words, as
the Scriptures say—and those prayers were
answered. For in the final weeks of her life, she
seemed reconciled. She seemed more peaceful. The
fight was gone. She finally seemed ready for it to
be over with.

From here, the story becomes one of mercy and
grace, where the God who longs to love us with an
incomprehensible love came through in a glorious
way only he can. For I believe Betty allowed him
into her heart to heal places and pains she'd not
given him before.

I sat with her in the hours before she died, and
that night the Lord provided several things to give
me peace. Mom was basically comatose, not
responsive, and breathing very slowly. The hospice
folks said, though, that hearing is the last thing to
go, so I talked to her, read Scriptures to her, and
prayed for her. I believe somehow, in a realm we
don't understand, my dear aunt Faith and
Mama Croxton were there on the other side, letting her know it was okay to let go. Watching
someone work through the transition into death is
a remarkable experience. Although her eyes were
closed, her eyebrows would lift as if in surprise,
and several times she smiled. The frown lines that
had been on her face for so many years seemed to
disappear as she neared the end of this life.

Later that night, about an hour before she
died, I was at home and in bed, somewhere
between awake and asleep. The Bible says God
will give us visions and dreams, and in my mind
I briefly saw my mother, dressed in a shining

*white robe. I firmly believe God gave me that
sight to reassure me I'd see her again someday.*

*Betty was a fighter. But eventually, even
fighters must retire. She has gone on now to
arrange the gardens in heaven and probably
organize a committee to improve something. In
closing, I'd like to read a Scripture that will
forevermore remind me of these past few years of
my mother's life and that I hope will mark my
life as well:*

*From 2 Timothy 4: "I have fought the good
fight, I have finished the race, I have kept the faith.
Now there is in store for me the
crown of righteousness, which the
Lord, the righteous Judge, will
award to me on that day—and not
only to me, but also to all who have
longed for his appearing" [vv. 7–8].*

*I hope that those crowns of
righteousness have holy chin straps,
because Betty will be so busy running around up there, hers will
fall off if she's not careful.*

*Thank you again for coming to
honor Miss Betty.*

> "MY MOST VIVID
> MEMORIES OF
> HIM ARE OF
> HIM LAUGHING."

The service to honor my father was beyond my expectations
as well. There were the hymns, prayers, and favorite Scripture
verses, but as befits a longtime musician with a history in
choir robes and wedding solos, the music at my father's service brought us all a little closer to heaven.

A longtime family friend, in his sixties by now, sang "How Great Thou Art." It was his trademark song and a favorite of my dad's. They had known one another since the 1950s and had sung together in choirs. He was honored to participate in this moment to honor my father.

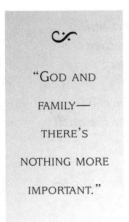

"GOD AND FAMILY— THERE'S NOTHING MORE IMPORTANT."

The sanctuary of my hometown church was filled with old and new friends and two rows of our dearest friends from Austin. As I rose to stand in the pulpit, where I'd read Scriptures and participated in services as a child, I felt my knees weaken and my heart sink. I didn't think I could ever get through this. In spite of all my training as a public speaker and my knowledge that eye contact with your audience is critical to success, I fixed my eyes on the empty balcony and shakily read my tribute to my father.

As I sat down, what seemed like six weeks later, the soloist approached the steps of the sanctuary. His booming voice filled the air and even now, well past retirement age, he needed no microphone. "O Lord my God. When I in awesome wonder ..." he began, and the tears started to flow. Thankfully, I'd had the foresight to speak before he sang. Afterward, I'd never have been able to get through these words:

> *Thank you for coming today to honor my dad.*
> *I'm a professional speaker and workshop*
> *leader and I know the importance of eye contact*
> *with the audience. However, getting through this*

today is requiring unprecedented reliance on the Holy Spirit and every bit of stage presence I ever learned, so I'm probably going to focus on the balcony where I'd sit as a preteen and eat candy during the service. Sorry, Clifford [my childhood pastor, who was there].

My father had the world's biggest hands and broadest shoulders and, of course, the longest, skinniest feet known to Larry's Shoes. I'd sit here in church as a little girl and lean on that shoulder and play with those hands. Those giant knuckles were like mountains and the wrinkles in his palm looked like rivers. He was to me a giant among men, and now, at the end of his life on earth, I've only begun to discover the great man he was to many others as well.

I always knew I adored him, but based on the cards and e-mails and calls I've gotten in the last eleven days, I wasn't alone. He was a joy to all he met. He was a great source of strength and stability to me throughout my entire life. My dad was rarely agitated, feathers rarely ruffled, and his love for me was always evident and unconditional, even when I nearly knocked the door off the station wagon backing out of the driveway or brought home a less-than-stellar grade in math.

He was fun and he was funny. My most vivid memories of him are of him laughing, usually at some joke he himself had just told. Even in his weakest moments, even

> ∽
>
> "I'VE LEARNED SO MUCH ABOUT HIM AND HIS PROVISION."

when his body was failing, he had a smile and a
one-liner for his friends and caregivers. During
the last two weeks of his life, he was mostly sleep-
ing and very confused, but occasionally, he'd
mumble something, then just chuckle to himself
and smile. He was one of the funniest people he
knew.

He never missed one of my performances,
whether at church or school. He always had time
for whatever projects I needed help with in spite
of his own hectic career and volunteer activities.
He and Mom always made sure I made it to
youth group or choir practice or musical practice
or whatever else was required to encourage my
spiritual development and channel my youthful
energy.

My father taught me essentials for living: how
to rewire a lamp, solder a circuit, use a drill and
a saw and a sander, plant a tree, drive a boat, tie
a cleat knot, put out a fire, paint a wall, and
basically putter my way through any problem. If
he and my mother together were anything, they
were remarkably practical.

"Beyond that, though, he and my grandmother, Mama Croxton, taught me both in
word and deed the importance of faith and
family. God and family—there's nothing more
important.

In his years at Ridglea Presbyterian Church,
he served on every conceivable committee, sang the
Messiah countless times, and demonstrated his
faith through his service as both a deacon and
elder. He had an unshakable belief that what will
be, will be, and that God has ordained it all.

[Which is a really loose translation of verses in Romans 8.]

Our extended family was together on every birthday. We cooked, we ate, we laughed, we played, and he and my uncles always fought over the last slice of Mama's pie. "The best one you ever made, Mama!" they'd say. He was incredibly devoted to his mother and younger sister as they faced the end of their days and deeply loved his other sister. (Olive June hates to be called the older sister or bigger sister, so we'll leave it at "other" sister.)

My father stuck with my mother through her illnesses and heartaches, committee meetings and city-council fights. Nothing about Betty Croxton was easy, but he was committed to her for life and lived out that life with grace and dignity.

Proverbs 3 says, "My son, do not forget my teaching, but keep my commands in your heart, for they will prolong your life many years and bring you prosperity. Let love and faithfulness never leave you; bind them around your neck, write them on the tablet of your heart. Then you will win favor and a good name in the sight of God and man."

Love and faithfulness were the hallmarks of Charlie Croxton. He loved his family, his friends, and never met a stranger. He faithfully loved

"OUR PRESENT SUFFERINGS ARE NOT WORTH COMPARING WITH THE GLORY THAT WILL BE REVEALED IN US."

God, loved to sing to him, and often couldn't get through the mealtime prayer at a family gathering without getting weepy. He had a good name in the sight of many men, and now he's receiving his reward in the sight of God.

This journey for me—of losing those I love down the inescapable passageway of death—really began in 1996 with the passing of my precious aunt Faith. Not long after, our sweet Mama Croxton went home at age 104. Then began my mother's lengthy battles with her slowly weakening body. When I learned how to write an obituary in freshman journalism classes at TCU, I had no idea I'd be called upon to use those skills so often. I'm tired, and I'm glad this season has come to an end.

I'm married to the only man in the world who could even begin to hold a candle to my dad. With my incredible husband and precious prayer-warrior friends at my side, I've struggled down a pothole-covered road filled with countless decisions, none of them easy.

Move or don't move? This apartment facility or that care center? Treat or don't treat and with what medication? Keep stuff or sell it? This doctor or that one? All the while, we've been slow dancing at death's door with countless "This is it—it could be any day now" phone calls.

When a long-expected death finally occurs, there's a surreal quality to it. Over the past week or two since he's died, I've still had moments where I thought, "Oh, gotta call and chat with Dad," even though we haven't been able to converse much in the past two months

leading up to his death. The reality of this passing will continue to sink in for us over the next
few weeks and months as we realize he's really
gone.

Our faith, though, will see us through. The
faith that was nurtured in these very halls has
already sustained me through a season of life I
could never have imagined. The prayers of friends
and family have upheld me. The Word of God has
given me life and hope when I've felt most desperate. But God has been faithful to carry me
through, and although it has not been at all easy,
I'm thankful for this season of my life where I've
learned so much about him and his provision for
both me and my parents.

It's often said that one's image of our heavenly Father is most influenced by our earthly
father. If that is true, then I had an advantage
from the start. My dad consistently modeled
what's recorded in Colossians 3: As one of God's
chosen people, holy and dearly loved, he clothed
himself with compassion, kindness, humility, gen-
tleness, and patience. He was willing to bear with
others and forgive, and over all those virtues, he
put on love.

The Word of God tells us that, because of
Christ's death on the cross for us, we can approach
God's throne with boldness. We can call him
"Abba." "Daddy." As I stood beside my father's
bed on May 12, watching him struggle to breathe
and push down that path toward death, I myself
cried, "Daddy! Abba, Father, bring your sweet
servant home."

Because of my faith in Christ and the faith of

*my family, I know that I know that I know I'll
see my earthly father again.*

*Our sweet little girl is named Karen Faith
after her beautiful aunt. That name is beginning
to be far more than just a name as she often dis-
plays a beyond-childlike faith in the Lord. When
things began to look bleak with her grandfather a
few weeks ago, she asked me, "Mom, does Pop
know Jesus?" "Yes," I told her, "he does. Why?" "I
just wanted to make sure I'd see him again," she
said matter-of-factly, and she skipped off to play.*

*Even now, the heavenly reunion party is still
going on with Papa Croxton and Mama and
Faith and Dad and my mom. Betty's probably
already fussed at him for taking so long to get
there. It's unfathomable to me, but I believe that
the stillborn son my mother bore two years before I
came along is now reunited with his parents in
some way we cannot imagine.*

*I have no idea what heaven looks like. If there
are committees, Betty's running one; and if there's
a choir, my dad is singing again; and if there's a
lake, he's fishing with Peter. I do know what the
Bible says in Romans 8:18: "I consider that our
present sufferings are not worth comparing with
the glory that will be revealed in us." And later,
in verses 38–39, "For I am convinced that neither
death nor life, neither angels nor demons, neither
the present nor the future, nor any powers, neither
height nor depth, nor anything else in all creation,
will be able to separate us from the love of God
that is in Christ Jesus our Lord."*

*Charlie Croxton lives on in that glorious love
of God. He lives on in his namesake grandson*

(who, by the way, just discovered his singing voice and golf swing, not unlike his pop). He lives on in the bright blue eyes and beautiful spirit of our daughter. Yes, he leaves behind the legacy of a loving family, but more important, my dad lives on in the hope of glory we all have if we know God.

I couldn't have walked the path I've half-walked, half-crawled without the Lord. Today, I not only honor and remember the sweet, sweet father who taught me that faith, but the sweet, sweet heavenly Father to whom I owe all the glory.

For anyone here today who doesn't have a personal, vibrant, and growing relationship with the God of the universe, who loves us deeply and has a plan for our lives, I encourage you to explore him in depth. Jesus said in John 3, "For God did not send his Son into the world to condemn the world, but to save the world through him." That is the reason for my hope and the source of hope for all ages to come.

Appendix A: Helpful Web Sites

These Web sites offer resources, links to local agencies and services, decision-making guides, and a wealth of additional information to help those facing elder-care issues.

www.caps4caregivers.org
   A national organization, Children of Aging Parents, sponsors this guide for caregivers.

www.aplaceformom.com
   This is a national elder-care referral service.

www.n4a.org
   This is the site of the National Association of Area Agencies on Aging.

www.aahomecare.org

This is a site sponsored by the American Association for Homecare.

www.caringinfo.org

This is the consumer site for the National Hospice and Palliative Care Organization.

www.ssa.gov

This is the site for the Social Security Administration.

APPENDIX B: RECOMMENDED READING

Briggs, Lauren Littauer. *The Art of Helping: What to Say and Do When Someone Is Hurting.* Colorado Springs: Life Journey/Cook Communications, 2003.

Kübler-Ross, Elisabeth, M.D. *On Death and Dying.* New York: Simon and Schuster/Touchstone, 1969.

Larimore, Walter L., M.D. *Complete Guide to Caring for Aging Loved Ones.* Carol Stream, IL: Focus on the Family/Tyndale House, 2004.

Strom, Kay Marshall. *A Caregiver's Survival Guide: How to Stay Healthy When Your Loved One Is Sick.* Downers Grove, IL: InterVarsity Press, 2000.

READERS' GUIDE

For Personal Reflection or
Group Discussion

READERS' GUIDE

This book delves deeply into the pain of impending loss, a pain you, the reader, most likely, understand all too well. But this book also imparts hope, the hope that it is possible to ease the heartache—at least a little—of a loved one's last days and the promise that God is faithful. This doesn't mean the pain vanishes, difficult decisions become easy, or the situation you face will be resolved quickly. It does mean, though, that God sees your quiet tears, hears the cries of your heart, and offers to comfort you. He'll also bring joy to your soul again—one day. And in the meantime, he'll guide you as you care for the ones he's entrusted into your care. Hopefully, this book will be a valuable part of that process.

The following questions are intended as a guide to help you think through some of the important issues raised in this book. As you go through the guide, you may want to dig more deeply into some of the questions and skim over those that seem irrelevant to your situation. That's expected, as everyone's experiences differ. Simply allow the issues raised to inspire your thoughts. Also, don't rush. There often aren't easy answers. Think through your response and reflect on it awhile. While an immediate answer may come to mind, the conclusions you reach after additional thought may prove to be the most beneficial.

Having said this, many families find that the end of a loved one's life can bring conflict or pain into various relationships. When taking the suggested steps, proceed prayerfully and cautiously if this is a possibility in your family. Also, please remember that expert advice may be required for some of the legal and medical decisions prompted by this guide.

Additionally, it may be useful to talk to a professional counselor about some of the emotional issues you are facing. Let the following questions guide you in discovering those areas where you may need further assistance, and don't hesitate to seek that help.

Finally, some questions reflect the pain of losing a loved one, and others the faithfulness of God. Allow him to use them to help you through this time. He knows and understands—he lost a loved one, too. His loss (and subsequent gain), however, brings us hope and peace, even as we find ourselves slow dancing at death's door.

CHAPTER 1

1. In what ways has God prepared you to care for your parents as they age? In what ways are you still not ready? How can you begin to work through those issues?

2. The author was struck by the realization that a person's identity is in Christ, not in his or her past. How can such an understanding alter a person's perspective on his childhood? How might it change her relationships with family members? Why can this truth be difficult to apply? In what ways can it bring freedom?

3. How does God demonstrate the balance between loving someone and not approving of his or her behavior? How can we find the same balance? Where does forgiveness fit into the picture?

4. a) Romans 8:28 states, "And we know that in all things God works for the good of those who love him, who have been called according to his purpose." What events in your life have made believing this promise difficult? What times in your life have proved it to be true?

   b) Isaiah 40:31 says, "Those who hope in the LORD will renew their strength," and Philippians 4:13 promises, "I can do everything through him who gives me strength." How have you seen God provide the strength and support you need to accomplish difficult tasks? When have you most needed that support?

Chapter 2

1. Why is it challenging to accept that our parents weren't (and aren't) perfect? In what ways have you felt disappointed or let down by your parents? What would explain their behavior or choices in their minds? How can you seek to understand your parents better?

2. If you hold anger or bitterness toward your parents, how do those attitudes hinder your relationship? Why is it important to work through such emotions and heal the relationship? What actions can you take to fix any breaches?

3. Why might someone not want to forgive his or her parents? Are there ever valid reasons? What benefits does forgiveness bring to our relationships with our parents as they age? How can you work toward forgiveness if you need to?

4. Peter admonished in 1 Peter 3:9, "Do not repay evil with evil or insult with insult, but with blessing, because to this

you were called so that you may inherit a blessing." How can you begin to overcome the pain of the past by blessing those who have hurt you? What blessings might you receive in return for taking steps to honor and love your parents in their later years?

CHAPTER 3

1. Paul said in 2 Corinthians 12:10, "When I am weak, then I am strong."

    a) Consider a time when you were at your weakest. What events or circumstances made it difficult to stay strong? What does it really mean that *God* is strong when *we* are weak?

    b) Reflect on a time when God was strong for you when you couldn't be. What, if anything, made that moment different from times when you haven't felt his strength? If you haven't seen God's strength in your life, how can you begin to find it?

2. Are there times when you feel God can't work in or through you? Describe the power of God, and honestly list the things that seem beyond his power to change. In what ways does your heart agree or disagree with the Bible's teaching about God's power? What might it take for you to believe God's promise?

3. How is it a comfort to realize that God knows all about the hurts of your past? Why is it difficult to accept that they were allowed? Why do we sometimes hide rather than allow God to begin fixing things now?

4. Psalm 126:5 says, "Those who sow in tears will reap with songs of joy." What promises do we have when we give our pain to God, allow him to work in and through us, and trust that he can and will transform our circumstances? Why do we sometimes miss the healing and peace God can bring?

CHAPTER 4

1. a) What benefits does a will bring on a personal (not just a legal) level? Why do people neglect this document? What concerns, if any, do you have for your family if your parents don't have an up-to-date will?

   b) What would you consider to be the most painful medical decision you may have to make for your parents? In honesty, how easy or difficult would you find it to be to make an end-of-life decision? How might legal or medical directives help?

2. What responsibilities does a child have when his or her parents can no longer care for themselves? If your parents

needed part-time care, what would you do? What about full-time care? If you have siblings, what are their expectations about your parents' care? At what point might you use tough love to ensure your parents are healthy and safe?

3. Obviously, these are difficult issues to discuss. What excuses do people make for putting them off? Are those reasons ever valid? Have you discussed with your loved ones the financial and medical issues raised by this chapter? What will it take for you to do so?

4. God commands us to "honor [our] father and [our] mother" (Ex. 20:12). How does planning for their care and/or passing help fulfill this command? What does it look like to honor them when you don't agree with the choices they're making for their finances or health care? How might making these decisions early free us to effectively love our parents during their last days?

CHAPTER 5

1. a) What legal benefits does a will provide? What, if any, would be a valid reason not to create a will? How might power-of-attorney documents be useful in your situation (if at all)? What is your opinion on getting legal assistance in creating such documents?

   b) Which of your parents' belongings mean the most to
      you? What are their most cherished possessions? What
      do you believe their wishes for those items would be?
      What would be the implications if your understanding
      is wrong?

2. What are your loved ones' desires should they require life
   support? What constitutes "life support" to you? What
   about to them? How are documents such as living wills and
   do-not-resuscitate orders comforting and empowering?

3. a) In what situations would it be appropriate to appoint a
      guardian over an elderly person? Who would the
      guardian be for your parents? What would their specific
      responsibilities be?

   b) How comfortable are you with the idea of hospice care
      or, in less challenging situations, with in-home assis-
      tance? What responsibilities are you comfortable having
      help with and which ones do you feel you can handle
      yourself?

4. a) The Bible has much to say about the stewardship of
      money. (See Matt. 6:24; 25:14–30; Luke 6:38;
      16:10–13.) How do stewardship responsibilities apply
      when it comes to caring for your parents? How can you
      fulfill those obligations?

b) Scripture also has a lot to say about the value of life. (See Ex. 20:13; Ps. 139:13–16; Jer. 1:5.) How do the various medical directives help us value life? Can they ever be used in a way that devalues life? If so, how? When is giving medical assistance valuing life, and at what point should we accept that God is calling his child home?

CHAPTER 6

1. How does the way you honor your parents change as you get older? What new actions can you take to demonstrate your care and respect?

2. In what ways is the call to provide for our parents harder today that in past centuries? In what ways is it easier? How does your heart respond to the thought of providing for them? What does it mean to "provide" in your situation?

3. Ultimately, planning and organizing free us to love our aging parents. How does each step of planning (wills, medical directives, physical care) and preparing (healing relationships, overcoming the past) allow us to better love them? What practical thing can you do for your parents that would show your love?

4. First Timothy 5:4 states, "If a widow has children or grandchildren, these should learn first of all to put their religion into practice by caring for their own family and so repaying their parents and grandparents, for this is pleasing to God." In what ways does caring for our parents put our faith into practice? What biblical teachings (directly or indirectly related to the family) do we fulfill when caring for our parents physically, financially, and emotionally?

CHAPTER 7

1. Journaling can sometimes be a helpful way to pour our hearts out to God and see his hand at work. How do you work through the challenging moments of life and the emotions they bring? What outlet do you have for the things on your heart? If journaling isn't for you, what alternatives will you employ?

2. Why is it important to spend time for ourselves when caregiving? What can make this difficult to do? What can happen if we don't? How can we address the guilt we often feel or that others place on us?

3. Why is it easy to neglect relationships with those closest to us when caring for a loved one? Why is it essential to

nurture these relationships? What does it mean to listen to our heart and pay attention to our conscience and the Holy Spirit when making decisions about our priorities?

4. Focusing on ourselves from time to time can feel selfish. Yet, Jesus often got away or spent time just with those closest to him when his life was the most chaotic. Read the following Bible verses, and pray for wisdom in caring for yourself: Matthew 14:23; 17:1; 21:17; Mark 1:35; Luke 4:42; 5:16; 6:12.

CHAPTER 8

1. How can you encourage and assist elderly loved ones to maintain their sense of identity as their living situations change? Why is this important?

2. Why do older people find it difficult to accept the assistance of those caring for them? As a loved one moves toward greater and greater care, how can we foster his or her independence in each situation?

3. It's often easy to push older people to do things that are growing increasingly difficult for them. It's also hard to

accept that they may be weakening. What signs can we watch for to help guide us in knowing when to encourage them to remain active and when to respect their limits?

4. Paul wrote of using our spiritual gifts for building the body of Christ in 1 Corinthians 12. In what ways can older and even physically failing loved ones still use their spiritual gifts for the benefit of others? How is it beneficial to them and to those around them when they do so? How can we encourage them to utilize the gifts God has given them, regardless of their circumstances?

CHAPTER 9

1. What does it mean to "protect our hearts" in the midst of caregiving? Name several steps you can take—today or this week—to nurture your heart and soul.

2. The author strongly encourages us to protect our hearts, yet she also highlights the importance of working through the pain and heartache of the past. How is it possible to do both? In what ways might each suggestion help you better fulfill the other?

3. Why is it spiritually important to protect or guard our hearts? Why would Solomon command it in Proverbs 4:23? In what ways is it apparent that God does care about your heart? How do you handle the times when it doesn't feel like he cares?

4. Psalm 69:32 says, "May your hearts live." In what ways can our hearts live in the events surrounding a loved one's death? How can our relationship with God help keep our hearts alive? What does it mean, on a spiritual level, for our hearts to "live"? What does it mean on a practical, daily-life level?

CHAPTER 10

1. How can items such as photographs help us connect with others and give renewed strength during a difficult time? How can you begin to collect the stories behind your treasured family photos?

2. In what ways are scrapbooks helpful in sorting through and passing on family history? What is the benefit in gathering the information into one place rather than leaving it scattered? If scrapbooking isn't for you, what other ways can you think of to help put keepsakes in a usable order?

3. Name several items from your family home that are meaningful to you. How do they help tell your family's history?
   How can they best be used to pass the legacy on to future
   generations? What are you keeping to pass on from your
   own life?

4. The Israelites regularly set up altars. (See Gen. 12:7; 33:20;
   Judg. 6:24.) While often functional, they also served as
   reminders of God's faithfulness in specific situations. How
   can the mementos of our families be like altars and help
   serve as reminders to us and future generations of what
   God has done in our families?

CHAPTER 11

1. What negative family legacies (unhealthy behaviors,
   ungodly attitudes) do you want to stop? How can you
   start a new and godly family trait to pass along? Why are
   these questions important as our parents reach the end of
   their lives?

2. Name several family traditions you'd like to keep. What are
   you doing to preserve them? Similarly, what character qual-
   ities of your parents do you value? How can you develop
   these in yourself? Why are these questions important as our
   parents reach the end of their lives?

3. How can you begin to collect and preserve your family history? What are some of the most pressing questions you have about your loved ones, and how can you find answers? As you consider your gifts, talents, and hobbies, how can you use them to pass on your family history?

4. Psalm 89:1 says, "I will make your faithfulness known through all generations." Why is it important to share the story God is weaving in our families? Summarize the ways God's faithfulness has been shown in your family (even if it is his hand bringing you out of or through some negative events).

CHAPTER 12

1. What are some specific stories about your parents or extended family that clearly illustrate God's faithfulness? How can you begin to share this history? Whom will you tell?

2. Sometimes God's goodness to us can be seen through negative issues or events. What has God brought your family out of? Which stories illustrate how far your family, your parents, or even just you have come in Christ?

3. What might prevent us from honestly looking at the spiritual legacy of our family? What can we gain by delving into this aspect of the past?

4. Deuteronomy 11:18–21 speaks of the absolute importance of sharing the truths of God with coming generations. How can knowing our families' histories help us in sharing the gospel?

CHAPTER 13

1. After such a drawn-out waiting for her mother's death, the author struggles with feelings of wanting the ordeal over. In what ways can you relate? During her mom's final moments of life, the face that had been so battered by illness was transformed. What do you think was happening? What might the dying woman have been seeing and saying?

2. As her dad neared the end of his life, the author needed to decide whether to get away for a day or two. What would you have done? Again, her father's countenance changes in his last moments and he smiles. Do you think this is just a natural occurrence, or is something else more spiritual happening? Why?

3. The author considers the reunion of her parents with each other and with family members. What do you believe heaven is like? What of your understanding of heaven is from the Bible? From others? What aspects of heaven bring the most comfort to you?

4. This book relates a long, drawn-out, and difficult time of loss. Yet the author concludes with 1 Corinthians 15:55–57: "Where, O death, is your victory? Where, O death, is your sting? ... Thanks be to God! He gives us the victory...." How can she say this? What in her story demonstrates that God really was faithful in such a difficult situation? What, if anything, would it take for you to honestly thank God for the victory he's given?

The Word at Work Around the World

A vital part of Cook Communications Ministries is our international outreach, Cook Communications Ministries International (CCMI). Your purchase of this book, and of other books and Christian-growth products from Cook, enables CCMI to provide Bibles and Christian literature to people in more than 150 languages in 65 countries.

Cook Communications Ministries is a not-for-profit, self-supporting organization. Revenues from sales of our books, Bible curricula, and other church and home products not only fund our U.S. ministry, but also fund our CCMI ministry around the world. One hundred percent of donations to CCMI go to our international literature programs.

CCMI reaches out internationally in three ways:

• Our premier International Christian Publishing Institute (ICPI) trains leaders from nationally led publishing houses around the world.

• We provide literature for pastors, evangelists, and Christian workers in their national language.

• We reach people at risk—refugees, AIDS victims, street children, and famine victims—with God's Word.

Word Power, God's Power

Faith Kidz, RiverOak, Honor, Life Journey, Victor, NexGen — every time you purchase a book produced by Cook Communications Ministries, you not only meet a vital personal need in your life or in the life of someone you love, but you're also a part of ministering to José in Colombia, Humberto in Chile, Gousa in India, or Lidiane in Brazil. You help make it possible for a pastor in China, a child in Peru, or a mother in West Africa to enjoy a life-changing book. And because you helped, children and adults around the world are learning God's Word and walking in his ways.

Thank you for your partnership in helping to disciple the world. May God bless you with the power of his Word in your life.

For more information about our international ministries, visit www.ccmi.org.

Additional copies of *SLOW DANCING AT DEATH'S DOOR*
and other Life Journey titles are available
wherever good books are sold.

If you have enjoyed this book,
or if it has had an impact on your life,
we would like to hear from you.

Please contact us at:

LIFE JOURNEY
Cook Communications Ministries, Dept. 201
4050 Lee Vance View
Colorado Springs, CO 80918

Or at our Web site: www.cookministries.com

LIFE JOURNEY®
Bringing Home the Message for Life